Thoroughbred and Other Ponies

Painted by A. Cooper, R.A.   Engraved on wood by F. Babbage.

THE SHOOTING PONY.

THOROUGHBRED
AND OTHER PONIES

WITH REMARKS ON THE HEIGHT OF
RACEHORSES SINCE 1700

Being a Revised Edition of

PONIES: PAST AND PRESENT

BY

SIR WALTER GILBEY, Bart.

ILLUSTRATED

VINTON & CO., Ltd.
9, NEW BRIDGE STREET, LONDON, E.C.

—

1903

PREFACE TO THE SECOND EDITION.

The first edition of this book, published in August, 1900, being out of print, advantage has been taken of the demand for a second issue to make certain additions and alterations to the original text.

The Chapter on the Height of Horses and the relations of Height to Utility has been added.

Some notes on the Galloways of the South of Scotland, on Highland Ponies and on Arabs have been also added; the last with special reference to the prominent part played by Eastern horses in laying the foundations of our modern breed of racehorses.

Elsenham Hall, Essex.
May, 1903.

CONTENTS.

ILLUSTRATIONS.

THOROUGHBRED AND OTHER PONIES.

WITH REMARKS ON THE

HEIGHT OF RACEHORSES SINCE 1700

HEIGHT OF EARLY RACEHORSES

IT is worthy of remark that we rarely find in Turf history any particulars of the height of any horse unless he were exceptionally small or exceptionally big. Since it became the fashion to aim at producing a long-striding animal, there has been a general tendency to describe horses as bigger than they were; unless they were below the average height, when there has been a tendency to minimise their height in order to make their performances appear the more remarkable

We shall probably be right in assuming that about the year 1700 our racehorses averaged not more than 14 hands. The three imported horses—the Byerly Turk (imported 1689), the Darley Arabian (imported 1706), and the Godolphin Arabian (imported 1724)—to which

1

so many of our modern thoroughbreds trace their descent, were all animals of 14 hands or a little more, and nowhere do we find complaint that they lacked anything in point of size.

Mixbury (see p. 124), got by Curwen's Bay Barb (imported in Charles II.'s reign) out of a mare by Old Spot, measured 13 hands 2 inches.

Turf records contain the conditions for a Plate, value 6 guineas, run for at Newmarket in 1711 ; each horse, mare, or gelding was to carry 10 stone if 14 hands high, if above or under allowed weight for inches. In 1750 a £50 Plate was offered at Newmarket, "14 hands to carry 8 stone 7 lb" Obviously 14 hands was the normal or average height of the racehorse of that period.

Again, the conditions for Give-and-Take Plates framed in 1770 provide a scale of the weights to be carried by horses of from 12 to 15 hands. Obviously 15 hands was the extreme height for which it was thought necessary to provide, as 12 hands was the least , either extreme was probably rarely reached.

Admiral Rous (writing in *Baily's Magazine* in 1860) showed that the average height of our thoroughbreds had increased one inch in every twenty-five years , and we find no difficulty in proving the accuracy of the statement

HEIGHT OF THE RACEHORSE ABOUT A D. 1800.

About the end of the 18th century the practice of racing two-year-olds was introduced,
bringing with it the inevitable process of
"forcing" the growth of young stock   The
author of *A Comparative View of the Form
and Character of the English Racer and Saddle
Horse during the Past and Present Centuries,*
published in 1836, has much to say concerning
the increased height of racehorses, which by
that date had altered the character of the breed
He says :—

"We have seen that the 'Turf' commenced with
ponies, and that for a long period horses under 14 hands
were found among the best racers   The intelligent reader must perceive that the great size so much
admired by the public in brood mares has been acquired
.   The English racer, we cannot doubt, acquired
his enlarged structure by rich food "

The excessive increase in height which
the author deprecates had produced increased
speed, but the horses of the thirties could not,
in his opinion, be compared with those of fifty
years previously for stoutness, for ability to
carry weight, and for staying power ; yet it is
very doubtful whether the average height of
the racehorse at the time this work was written
exceeded 15 hands. At the beginning of the
century, say 1801-20, the process of development had not gone so far, and if we put the

average height of the racehorse at that time at
14 hands 3 inches we shall have much evidence
to support us.

HEIGHT OF THE MODERN RACEHORSE.

Though there are horses which measure as
much as 16 hands 2 inches or even 16 hands
3 inches on the Turf and at the stud to-day,
it will be safe, taking into account the smaller
stature of the mare, to put the average height
of the modern thoroughbred at 15 hands $2\frac{1}{2}$
inches. "So excellent an authority as the late
Matthew Dawson," says Mr Charles Richardson in *The English Turf*, "considered it to be
demonstrable that within the experience of
living persons the size of the racehorse has
increased in this country.'

This practically confirms Admiral Rous's
assertion. From an average height of 14
hands in the year 1700 the breed has been
graded up to an average of 15 hands $2\frac{1}{2}$ inches
in the year 1900. How much this means is
best shown by the diagrams on the opposite
page which represent the size of the horse,
14 hands, in 1700; the size of the horse, 14
hands 3 inches, in 1800, and the size of the
modern thoroughbred, 15 hands $2\frac{1}{2}$ inches, in
1900

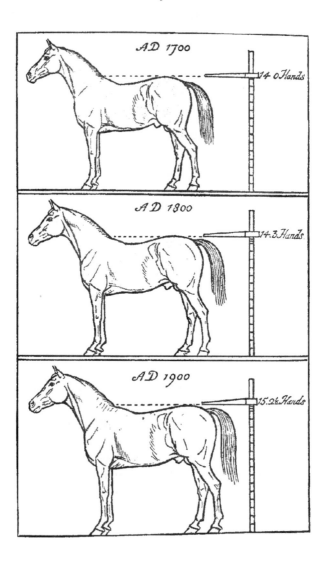

HEIGHT AND UTILITY.

I — IN THE RACEHORSE.

" A good big one will always beat a good little one," said the famous John Scott to the late Sir Tatton Sykes in the hearing of the Hon Francis Lawley, and the saying has taken rank as an axiom of racing. But before we accept the saying as a last word in favour of big horses over small ones we must look a little more closely into facts

Mr. William Day, in *The Racehorse in Training*, says —

" A really good big horse is probably better than a really good small one, but as a rule you may get fifty good small horses for one good large one, and the former will, and do, run well after the latter has been put to the stud . . A good big horse may beat a good little one over a short course, or even at a mile or so ; but I think at three or four miles a good little one would beat the best big one I ever saw "

Mr. Day goes on to cite the performances of Camarine, Venison, Touchstone, Joe Miller, and other small horses, but he quite admits the merits of such big ones as Fisherman and Rataplan. Taking the average height of the thoroughbred mares and entire horses at 15 hands 2½ inches, it would seem that we have had fifty stout runners below that height for one that exceeded it.

Nor does the good big horse commend himself as superior to the good little one at the stud Mr Day, in *The Horse · How to Breed and Rear Him*, after reviewing his long experience, says .—

" I think it will be plainly seen that little stallions with mares suited to them do get good stock and much better than most large horses get .   . the comparison exhibited in the above illustrations of the successes of small and large stallions at the stud must, I think, be allowed to be very much in favour of the former .   . Indeed, the only instance that I can call to mind within the last forty years of a thorough good stallion above or about 16 hands was Stockwell "

Stockwell, as racing men will remember, was far from being a typical big horse , he stood on short legs, and his bulk caused him to be frequently compared to a dray horse

We may therefore accept it as proved that excessive height is not an advantage to the racehorse as a breed , though the hope of producing the "good big one" which will beat a "good little one" over the short distances of present-day racing will, we may be sure, induce men to continue aiming at great height.

II.—IN THE STEEPLECHASER.

A steeplechase horse is required to perform much harder work than the flat racer. He must be able to go farther, to carry a heavier

weight, to possess greater activity, and (what
creates demand for greater soundness of limb
and constitution) he very frequently continues
carrying silk till twelve or fourteen years old

My friend the Hon Francis Lawley, whose
unrivalled personal knowledge of racing ex-
tending over more than fifty years enabled him
to speak with authority, wrote me on this
subject only a short time before his death, on
September 17th, as follows concerning winners
of the Liverpool Grand National —

"The Grand National at Liverpool has been won by
a larger number of little horses than of big ones. For
instance, Mr. Osborne's Abd-el-Kadr, who won twice
(1850 and 1851), and ought to have won thrice, was
barely 15 hands. Lord Poulett's The Lamb,* who won
twice (1868 and 1871), was about the same size as
Abd-el-Kadr. Casse Tête (1872) was a small mare ;
and many other winners of this typical 'chase, such
as Regal (1876), Shifnal (1878), Empress (1880), Volup-
tuary (1884), Old Joe (1886), and, I believe, Father
O'Flynn (1892), were small. The same, I believe, may
be said of Lord Coventry's pair, Emblem (1863) and
Emblematic (1864). Perhaps the best 'chaser that ever
negotiated a big country—The Chandler, who was
almost as old when he won the Grand National against
a formidable field as was his rider, Captain Little—was
what the Captain always called 'a big little one', that
is to say, he stood on short legs

"When the race in question has been won by big
horses such as Lottery (1839) and The Colonel (1869
and 1870), they did not go so fast over the course as
smaller animals did , but it must be considered that The

* The Lamb was only 14 hands 2 inches

Colonel was a superb specimen of the British thoroughbred. . . . To sum up, few heavyweights who have
gone straight and well across country will fail to tell
you that, walking 15 stone or more, they have been
better carried by a small horse than by a big one, the
latter will tire sooner. The great Earl of Jersey, who
was at one time invincible for the Two Thousand
Guineas and who won three Derbys, used to sneer at a
big hunter, who (as he said) 'could not carry himself
and how can he carry me?' The grandfather of the
present Viscount Valentia, who was universally known
as 'the Laird,' rode 16 stone and invariably was
mounted on small horses."

III.—IN THE HUNTER AND SADDLE HORSE

We seek in the hunter and saddle horse
strength to carry weight, staying power to
perform long and trying journeys, with soundness of constitution and limb. Height in
itself is no advantage whatever, and, being
too frequently due to disproportionate length
of limb, great height is, speaking generally, a
defect The qualities we desire in the hunter
are usually found in the short-legged, short-
backed animal—in a word, the compact horse
—and any hunting man of experience will
admit that the best hunters he has known have
been horses of not over 15 hands 2 inches. In
the hunter we need the maximum of activity
with as much speed as we can obtain without
sacrificing other essential qualities; and the
additional inches which at the cost of strength

confer greater speed on the racehorse are a
distinct objection in the hunter No horse
is more severely tried as to wind, and it is
well known that big horses are far more liable
to turn roarers than the small, compact horse.
The anonymous author of the work on the
English Racer and Saddle Horse, published
in 1836, says —

" We want in saddle horses a larger skeleton and a
greater aggregate amount of muscular power than we
find in the natural animal, but we must unite with
these factitious properties as much of the vigour and
activity of the natural animal as is practicable   .   .
We find the symmetry of the skeleton in the enlarged
bone best adapted for useful purposes when it diverges
least from the natural—from that form which we call
compact   Horses which are able to traverse a great
distance rapidly and frequently with a considerable
weight upon their backs display this form.   This, like
stoutness, is an effect, and one which Nature only can
produce.   Large horses can only be reared on very
unnatural food, they are less stout than small ones
under exertion, take more time to recover from this,
and do not carry weight so well, in other words, stoutness and the power of carrying much weight for a long
distance at a rapid rate are not dependent on the
comparative weight or surface of the muscles, but on
a sufficiency of muscles, united with that distribution
of the skeleton which, while it denotes vigour, is
mechanically adapted for fine action and for carrying
weight "

It is to be borne in mind that this was
written at a period when the saddle horse
was in far more general use for road travel
than it has been since the spread of railroads ;

it was written in days when the saddle horse was still used to make long journeys and was esteemed in accordance with his ability to carry his rider comfortably and easily at all paces day after day.

IV.—IN THE CARRIAGE HORSE.

For work we put our trust in the small, compact horses of from 15 hands to 15 hands 3 inches, as we know from experience that the smaller horses will go farther, will recover more quickly from the effects of fatigue, and will stand the strain of continuous work better than the over-sized animals.

We must not, perhaps, regard the carriage horse from a strictly utilitarian standpoint. The London barouche and carriage horses are esteemed, in the majority of cases, for their appearance rather than for working qualities, and Fashion has decreed that the horses for such purposes should stand 16 hands, preferably 16 hands 1 inch or more. The actual work demanded of such horses is not great, but it is the most trying to health of any that horses in civilised countries are required to perform, housed too often in a stable heated beyond the point sanctioned by the good horse-master, carriage horses are kept standing about the streets exposed to all weathers.

It says much for their inherent soundness
that they endure as they do endure. At the
same time the big, upstanding carriage horse
from 16 to 16 hands 2 inches is not the
animal we select when long and frequent
journeys are to be made

THE RATE OF NATURAL GROWTH.

It is a curious fact that in all the enormous
mass of literature dealing with horses, their
breeding and management, the rate of growth
in the young animal has nowhere, so far as
the present writer's researches have shown,
received attention   Professor Cossar Ewart in
the course of an article* on this subject gave
some interesting figures bearing on the subject , apart from these the only details that a
good deal of search has revealed are contained
in a letter addressed by the same authority to
the *Field* of June 17th, 1899. These relate
to a thoroughbred foal whose sire and dam
both exceeded 15 hands 2 inches, and they
show the height at various stages to be as
follows —

Height at Birth	At Two months.	At Six months	At One year
9·0¼	10·3	11·3½	13

* See *Live Stock Journal Almanac*, 1901   Vinton and
Co , Ltd

In reply to inquiries on the subject, Professor Ewart kindly informs me that this foal—

"did very badly the first year, mainly, I think, because the dam was out of condition and never able to nourish him properly. A foal having 14-hand parents, if well nourished by the dam and given a reasonable amount of food during the first winter, often measures at the end of the first year 53 inches (13 hands 1 inch) at the withers. At the end of the third year this foal measured 60 inches (15 hands) at the withers. During the second and third years he recovered lost ground just as children recover ground lost during illness. Part of the gain during the second and third years should perhaps be ascribed to the foal being gelded when fourteen months old—gelding predisposing to an increase in the length of the legs and to growth of the spinal processes which enter into the formation of the withers. No attempt was ever made to force the growth of the foal."

ARTIFICIAL PROMOTION OF GROWTH.

The growth of the young horse may be promoted or checked, within certain limits. The practice of racing two-year-old horses has brought in its train various evils, of which "forcing" young stock for the sale-ring is by no means the least. The existence of the young racehorse is artificial from his birth. The breeder, for the sale-ring at all events, aims at getting his foals as soon after January 1st as possible; thus the foal makes his appearance when there is no fresh growth of grass to nourish his dam, and when he must spend the greater part of his days in a close stable. To quote from Mr Charles Richardson's excellent book, *The English Turf* :—

" —it is the object of the public breeder to send his youngsters into the ring as big as possible Now, in order to have a yearling really big at eighteen months old or less, it must be forced, and it is this unnatural forcing which causes so many of the best-bred and best-looking of public yearlings to turn out failures on the racecourse Year after year one sees yearling colts sent into the ring nearer 16 than 15 hands high, and fillies half a hand less, whereas had these youngsters been brought up less artificially they would certainly have averaged nearly a hand less in height at that period of their existence. In addition to being overgrown in the matter of inches, many of them have been fed on soft food until they are far too fat, and thus their worst points are often completely hidden."

This forcing process probably does not affect the height to which the horse ultimately grows He does not, under these conditions, reach a greater stature than he would do if reared naturally , but he reaches his maximum size earlier. The result appears in another direction : his constitution is adversely affected, and when subjected to the hard work of training and racing he " goes to pieces " before he attains to maturity In this we have an example of carrying artificial promotion of growth to an injurious extreme.

NATURAL PROMOTION OF GROWTH.

Growth and development are very largely dependent on the pasture. In a little book * published a few years ago, to exemplify the benefit derived by horses from grazing on fresh and untainted grass, I referred to an experiment made with heavy horses; and may venture to reproduce here a few lines that appear germane to our subject .—

" The theory of fresh grazing has been tested by placing a certain number of mares, on return from service by the best sire money could procure, upon land where the pasture was not fresh, in the following year the same number of mares served by the same sire, under identically similar circumstances, have been placed on pastures which had been freshly laid down, or upon old grass land on which horses had not been grazed for several years The produce in the latter two cases have been to an extraordinary extent superior in bone, muscle, and condition to their brothers and sisters of the previous year I can attribute their superiority to nothing else than their 'Nature's' feeding These tests of the fresh-grazing theory have not been confined to one year, but have run over several years "

These tests serve to demonstrate the beneficial results of good *natural* feeding There was no idea of "forcing" the growth of the young stock; the object was simply to ascertain what degree of difference in nourishing

---

* *Young Racehorses (Suggestions for Rearing)*, by Sir Walter Gilbey, Bart Vinton and Co., Ltd. 1898

properties exists between pasture somewhat
tainted by horses and perfectly fresh pasture.
The results prove that bone, muscle, and constitution benefit by superior *natural* feed. I
am not prepared to say whether the young
animals gained anything in height; if they
did so, development in this direction was
quite in harmony with the development of
bone and muscle

CONTROL OF GROWTH

The great prices which have been paid in
recent years for polo ponies have naturally
been the means of compelling the attention
of breeders to an industry which may be
remunerative The greatest difficulty in the
breeder's way is that of height. For there
can be no certainty whatever that a small
sire will beget, or that a small mare of a race
normally big will throw, a foal which shall
" take after" his sire or dam in point of size,
and it is absolutely necessary, if success in
breeding small-sized animals is to attend the
breeder's efforts, to seek measures whereby
the natural growth may be checked without
impairing the many high qualities required in
ponies for the game of polo.

How undesired development may be successfully controlled with advantage to handi-

ness and robustness of constitution has
been shown by Mr Christopher Wilson, of
Rigmaden, to whose labours as a pony
breeder reference will be found on pp 79-80.
Hard living and exposure to weather, we
repeat, do not stimulate growth , the frame
of the animal adjusts itself to the conditions
under which it is supported, and Nature will
not sanction the development of the body
larger than she can maintain.

A passage from Professor Ewart's letter to
the writer refers to this point —

" I need not say that if the food is insufficient up to the
end of the third year, or, for that matter, up to the end
of the second year (but especially during the period of
adolescence, when the reproductive glands are matur-
ing), the growth will be permanently arrested. This is
especially true of the growth of the legs, which of necessity comes to a close when the end piece or pieces are
fused to the shaft of the long bones. Want of food may
for a time delay this fusion, but eventually, however
restricted the diet, coalescence sets in and permanently
arrests further increase in the length of the legs. There
is, however, no reason why growth should not continue
for several years at the withers. Short-legged horses
can be manufactred by stinting the food during the
first two years and feeding heavily during the next two "

POSSIBILITY OF APPLYING MR. WILSON'S METHODS.

Whether the methods so successfully employed by Mr. Christopher Wilson on animals
three-parts Hackney and one-part Fell pony
blood could be employed on young stock in

2

which racehorse blood replaced the Hackney is another matter. It is not to be expected that foals three-parts thoroughbred could be turned out with impunity, the constitution of the thoroughbred has been rendered so delicate by the superlatively artificial conditions of his life for generations that in all probability the first week of cold and wet spring weather would lay the foundations of lasting disease, if it did not kill him outright To treat him thus would be on a par with planting hothouse exotics out of doors in winter with the view of rendering them more healthy

Nevertheless, a modified form of this treatment might be productive of good results. The half bred dam and her three-quarter-bred foal could be reared under natural conditions not too severe, when, if the youngster survived, he would develop such a frame as the climate and the food within his daily reach warranted.

HIGHEST VITALITY AND VIGOUR ACCOMPANY NORMAL HEIGHT.

We may take it (1) that Nature prescribes a normal average of size for each breed of horse, such size depending greatly upon climate and conditions of existence, (2) that the degree of vitality with which the horse is endowed coincides with the normal frame of the animal and does not increase in ratio with the size to which the frame may be enlarged by man's devices; and (3) that when, by careful mating, rich feeding, and general pampering, the frame is abnormally enlarged, that larger frame is more liable to disease and more susceptible of injury from exposure or overwork.

Mr. Wilfrid Scawen Blunt, who for the last twenty years or more has devoted great attention to the breeding of pure Arabs, addressed to General Sir F. Fitzwygram a remarkably instructive letter, which appears as a postscript in the last edition of that well-known work, "Horses and Stables" Mr Blunt says that when he began to breed Arabs in England he began to do so with the view of grading them up to a larger size, that their excellent qualities might be increased in proportion with their size.

He found no difficulty in grading them up to a larger size, but having done so, he was at last forced to conclude that the bigger Arab was not better than the Arab of normal height —on the contrary, that the big one was not so good, and that nothing was gained and something was lost when the Arab was bred up over Nature's average of 14 hands 2 inches.

So convinced is Mr Blunt by the fruit of his long experience, that he now weeds out from his breeding stud all the animals that exceed the 14 hands 2 inches standard, at which height the Arab is proved to be at his best.

In another book* numerous examples are quoted of the great endurance and independence of luxury which have been exhibited by small horses in campaigns or travelling, in every part of the world. There can be no question whatever but that this superiority has been proved past challenge.

The report on the work of the Imperial Yeomanry in South Africa, issued by the War Office, brings fresh proof, if it were needed, that the small horse has been by far the most useful and enduring , the Basuto ponies and other small animals purchased in South Africa out-lived and out-worked all others

That the English, Argentine, Hungarian, and American remounts were heavily handicapped by being put to hard work while out of condition, cannot be denied ; but the grass-fed ponies procured locally could not have been in what a horse-master would consider hard condition, and their higher utility was, we need not doubt, due to the fact that they combined the maximum of vitality and vigour with a frame of normal size

* *Small Horses in Warfare*, by Sir Walter Gilbey, Bart. Vinton and Co., Ltd. 1900

THOROUGHBRED AND OTHER PONIES.

PONIES OF EARLY BRITAIN.

Brief reference has been made in a previous publication* to the early subjugation of the horse in Eastern countries by man, and it is unnecessary here to further touch upon that phase of our subject

The early history of the horse in the British Islands is obscure. The animal is not indigenous to the country, and some suppose that the original stock was brought to England many centuries before the Christian era by the Phœnician navigators who visited the shores of Cornwall to procure supplies of tin. However that may be, the first historian who rendered any account of our islands for posterity found here horses which he regarded as possessing exceptional merit.

Julius Cæsar, when he invaded Britain in the year 55 B.C., found its inhabitants not only well furnished with horses, but also very dexterous in their management. He was

---

* *Horses, Past and Present*, by Sir Walter Gilbey, Bart Vinton and Co, Ltd., London. 1900.

greatly impressed with the excellence of the animals used by the ancient Britons in their war chariots.

The favourable opinion of the British horse of those days, which has been recorded by Cæsar, was due to the strength and hardiness of the animals and not to their superior size. There can be no doubt but that they were very small by comparison with modern horses,[*] and it is doubtful whether the horses of Britain gained materially in stature, until the Saxons and Danes introduced sires of larger breeds from the Continent.

These being for military purposes would have been stallions without exception; and being larger than the British breed would have got stock of increased height when crossed with our native mares

This being the case, we are confronted with the difficulty of distinguishing between the horses and ponies of these early times, the chroniclers do not attempt to differentiate between "horse" and "pony" as we understand the terms The process of developing a big horse was necessarily a slow one, from the system, or want of system, which remained in vogue until the fifteenth century, and was

[*] See *The Great Horse or War Horse,* by Sir Walter Gilbey, Bart Third Edition, 1899 Vinton and Co., Ltd

still in existence in some parts of England
in Henry VIII 's time.

Lord Arthur Cecil has put forward an
ingenious theory to account for the small size
of the moor and forest ponies He believes
that in early times when England was very
thinly populated, and vast tracts of unreclaimed
park-like land were occupied only by wild
animals, the ponies, enjoying the run of rich
natural pastures, grew to a larger size. In
of course time the population spread steadily
over the country, taking up fresh areas of land,
and, naturally, chose the best and richest
pastures to enclose for their cattle and sheep.
By gradual steps, therefore, the good grazing
which produced large growth, became closed to
the droves of wild ponies, which of necessity
resorted to the wastes, where the feed is sparse
and innutritious, and on such diet lost their
former size and strength.

During a long period the greater portion of
the country lay under forest and waste, and it
was the practice to let those mares which were
kept solely for breeding purposes run at large
in the woodlands, unbroken and unhandled.

Doomsday Book contains frequent mention
of *equæ silvestres, equæ silvaticæ*, or *equæ
indomitæ*, when enumerating the live stock
on a manor ; and there is evidence to show
that these animals (always mares, it will be

observed) were under a modified degree of supervision. They were branded to prove their ownership, and during the summer selected mares appear to have been "rounded up" to an enclosure in the forest for service. Apart from this they ranged the country at large, strangers alike to collar and bridle.

It would be unreasonable to suppose that the mares which were employed in agricultural work were not also used for breeding; the surroundings of the farmer's mare in those days were not luxurious, but she undoubtedly enjoyed shelter from the rigours of winter and more nourishing food than her woodland sister. Hence it is probable that the first differences in size, make and shape among English horses may be traced to their domestic or woodland ancestry on the dam's side

The life led by these animals gave them hardiness of constitution, soundness of limb, surefootedness, and small stature, and we venture to think that the half-wild ponies England possesses to-day in the New Forest, Exmoor, Wales and the Fell country, are the descendants of the woodland stock which is frequently referred to in ancient records, and which in 1535 and 1541 Henry VIII. made vigorous attempts to exterminate

The law of 1535 (26 Henry VIII) declares .—

" For that in many and most places of this realm,
commonly little horses and nags of small stature and
value be suffered to depasture, and also to cover mares
and felys of very small stature, by reason whereof the
breed of good and strong horses of this realm is now
lately diminished, altered and decayed, and further is
likely to decay if speedy remedy be not sooner provided
in that behalf.

" It is provided that all owners or fermers of parks
and enclosed grounds of the extent of one mile in
compass shall keep two mares, apt and able to bear
foals of the altitude or height of 13 handfuls at least,
upon pain of 40s.

" A penalty of 40s is imposed on the Lords, Owners,
and Fermers of all parks and grounds enclosed, as is
above rehearsed, who shall willingly suffer any of the
said mares to be covered or kept with any Stoned
Horse under the stature of 14 handfuls."

This act applied only to enclosed areas, and
therefore would not affect the wild ponies in
any appreciable degree. but six years later
another Act was passed (32 Henry VIII, c.
13) which provided that—

" No person shall put in any forest, chase, moor,
heath, common, or waste (where mares and fillies are
used to be kept), any stoned horse above the age of two
years, not being fifteen hands high within the Shires
and territories of Norfolk, Suffolk, Cambridge, Buckingham, Huntingdon, Essex, Kent, South Hampshire,
North Wiltshire, Oxford, Berkshire, Worcester, Glouces-
ter, Somerset, South Wales, Bedford, Warwick, North-
hampton, Yorkshire, Cheshire, Staffordshire, Lancashire
Salop, Leicester, Hereford and Lincoln. And furthermore, be it enacted, that if in any of the said drifts
there shall be found any mare, filly, foal, or gelding
that then shall be thought not to be able nor like to
grow, to be able to bear foals of reasonable stature or

not able or like to grow to be able to do profitable
labours by the discretions of the drivers aforesaid or of
the number of them, then the same driver or drivers
shall cause the same unprofitable beasts   . every
one of them to be killed, and the bodies of them to be
buried in the ground, as no annoyance thereby shall
come or grow to the people, those near inhabiting or
thither resorting."

This enactment was of a more far-reaching
character than its forerunner, but how far it
proved effective is another matter. Laws
more nearly affecting the welfare of the people
were less honoured in the observance than
the breach in those days. The "shires and
territories" enumerated were those in which
greatest attention was paid to the breeding
of Great Horses, "profitable labours," in
those times, could only mean military service,
agricultural work, and perhaps pack transport.
For the first-named purpose the woodland
ponies were useless, the ponies were no doubt
used in the plough and harrow on poor and
light soils, and as pack animals ; but only, we
may suppose, by persons whose poverty pre-
vented them from obtaining stronger cattle

A quaint rhyme in Thomas Tusser's *Five
Hundred Points of Good Husbandry*, published in 1557, shows how our ancestors
endeavoured to get the weight and bulk
necessary for draught purposes in default of
the height they had not learned to develop

by judicious management and mating. Tusser
recommends early gelding of horses destined
for the saddle—"geld young to be light," but
"for cart do not do so"; and he goes on to
counsel postponement of the operation till
the horse shall have grown "lusty and fat."

In 1556, when Elizabeth was on the throne,
Thomas Blundeville, of Newton Flotman,
wrote a book on *Horses and Riding*, and
prefaced it by an "Epistle dedicatorie" to
Robert Lord Dudley, Master of the Horse,
which begins :—

"It would be the means that the Queen may not
only cause such statutes touching the breeding of
Horses upon Commons to be put in execution but
also that all such parks within the Realme as be in
Her Highnesse hands and meet for that purpose might
not wholly be employed to the keeping of Deer (which
is altogether without profit), but partly to the necessary
breeding of Horses for service [i e , military service]
whereof this Realme of all others at this instant hath
greatest need."

It would appear, therefore, that Henry's
law had become a dead letter, or something
very like it, within twenty-five years of its
finding place on the Statute Book. It was
afterwards repealed* in respect of certain
counties by Queen Elizabeth and James I

These various early edicts no doubt pro-

---

* See pp. 26 and 23, *Horses, Past and Present*, by Sir
Walter Gilbey, Bart. Vinton and Co., Ltd 1900

duced some result in the more central parts
of England, though, as we gather from Blundeville's " Epistle," those charged with their
administration failed to enforce them in areas
more remote. A certain amount of driving
and killing no doubt was done, but probably
no more than enough to make the herds
wilder than before and send them in search
of safety to the most inaccessible districts.

The natural result of this would be to
preserve the breeds in greater purity than
would have been the case had they been
allowed to intermingle with horses which, after
the harvest was carried, were turned out to
graze at will over the unfenced fields and
commons. It was worth glancing at these
items of horse legislation to discover that the
half-wild ponies have survived, not by grace
of man's aid or protection, but in defiance
of his endeavours to stamp them out.

Nearly a century later (1658) the Duke of
Newcastle published his elaborate and important work,* and therein urged strongly the
desirability of discouraging the breeding of
ponies. The records of subsequent reigns
show occasional endeavour to improve by
legislation the breeds of horses needed for

---

* *Feeding, Dressing and Training of Horses for the Great
Saddle.*

military purposes, tournaments, racing and
sport, but until we come to the time of George
II we find no *positive* attempt to discourage
the breeding of ponies. An Act passed in
1740 was definite enough in the purpose it
sought to attain. This was the suppression of
races by "poneys" and other small or weak
horses.

Under this law matches for prizes under £50
were forbidden, save at Newmarket and Black
Hambleton, and the weights to be carried by
horses were fixed at 10 stone for a five-year-
old, 11 stone for a six-year-old, and 12 stone
for a seven-year-old horse

The statute had two-fold intention : it was
framed " not only to prevent the encourage-
ment of a vile and paltry breed of horses, but
likewise to remove all temptation from the
lower class of people who constantly attend
these races, to the great loss of time and
hindrance of labour, and whose behaviour still
calls for stricter regulations to curb their
licentiousness and correct their manners."

The law does not appear to have put an end
to pony-racing altogether. In the *Gentleman's
Magazine* of July, 1797, " A Farmer," writes a
letter complaining of the injurious increase of
the smallest breed of ponies "which are no
kind of use." He says that these ponies are
only broken for racing purposes and considers

that the pony turf encouraged idleness and dissipation.

Before 1800, and during the last century, organised effort to improve these breeds has followed recognition of their possibilities for usefulness, and in few localities, if any, does the original stock remain pure. In Devonshire, Hampshire, Wales, Cumberland, the Highlands, Shetland, and in the West of Ireland, the original strains have been intermingled and alien blood introduced. Arab, Small Thoroughbred, and Norfolk Hackney sires have produced new and improved breeds less fitted to withstand the rigours of winter and the effects of scanty food contingent on independent and useless existence, but infinitely better calculated to serve the interests of mankind.

Before the establishment of the Hackney Horse Society in 1883 the dividing line between the horse and the pony in England was vague and undefined. It was then found necessary to distinguish clearly between horses and ponies, and accordingly all animals measuring 14 hands or under were designated "ponies," and registered in a separate part of the Stud Book.

The Royal Agricultural Society, in the year 1889, accepted the altered conditions as to height established by the Hackney Society in

1883 and framed on these lines the schedule of
classes at their show held that year in Windsor
Great Park. The dividing line thus drawn
between *Horse Classes* and *Pony Classes* in the
Windsor Prize list has been recognised at all
shows since that of 1889.

It may now be said that for all show purposes, save only the Polo Pony Society's Show,
all animals *over* 14 hands are officially considered as horses and eligible only for entry in
HORSE Classes, and that those measuring
14 hands or less are accepted as ponies and as
such eligible to compete only in PONY Classes

The Stud books, which now give full particulars of owners, breeders, and also the
heights of animals, serve to direct breeders
in their choice of sires and dams.

The altered Polo rule which fixes the limit of
height at 14 hands 2 inches may be productive
of some little confusion, but for all other
purposes 14 hands is the recognised maximum
height of a pony. Prior to 1883 small horses
were called indifferently galloways, hobbies,
cobs, or ponies, irrespective of their height.

Engraved on wood by F. Babbage.

A PONY HACK.

A pony well known on Newmarket Heath and North Country racecourses about 1828.

accruing from the droves of ponies from that
date till November, 1220, this donation being
for the benefit of the soul of his late father,
King John. Thus it is evident that the New
Forest ponies of the thirteenth century were
sufficiently numerous, and of a stamp sufficiently useful, to form a source of revenue to
the Crown.

The remote history of the breed need not
concern us, for it was not until comparatively recent times that any endeavour was
made towards the improvement of the
"forester," as it is called. The first infusion
of alien blood likely to be beneficial seems to
have been made about 1766 ; and the circumstances under which this fresh blood was
introduced are interesting

In 1750 H.R H. the Duke of Cumberland
acquired by exchange a thoroughbred foal
from his breeder, Mr. John Hutton The
animal was named Marske, and was run at
Newmarket: achieving no great success on
the turf, he was put to the stud, but up to the
time of the Duke's death his progeny had done
nothing to win reputation for their sire.

When the Duke died, in 1765, his horses
were sold at Tattersall's, and Marske was
knocked down "for a song" to a Dorsetshire
farmer The farmer kept him in the New
Forest district, and here Marske, the sire of

Eclipse, served mares at a fee of half-a-guinea,
till his famous son achieved celebrity. Eclipse
was foaled in 1764, won his first race on 3rd
May, 1769, at Epsom, and made his name in
a single season on the turf.

For four years at least, therefore (until Mr.
Wildman ferretted out "the sire of Eclipse"
and bought him for £20 to go to Yorkshire),
the New Forest breed of ponies were being
improved by the very best thoroughbred blood,
the effects of which continued to be apparent
for many years after Marske had left the
district.

It is at least probable that Marske ran in
the Forest during the lifetime of the Duke
of Cumberland; for that prince was Warden
of the New Forest, and evidence is forthcoming to show that he made a systematic
attempt to better the stamp of pony.

In this connection it must be borne in mind
that the thoroughbred of one hundred and fifty
years ago was what we should regard now as
a pony Admiral Rous, as stated on earlier
pages, has pointed out that the racehorse has
steadily increased in size since about 1700,
then the average height of the thoroughbred
was about 14 hands; Marske was under 14
hands 2 inches

For many decades after this infusion of
thoroughbred blood into the New Forest

stock by Marske nothing was done to maintain the improvement made. On the contrary,
the demand for ponies increased, and the commoners took advantage of the higher prices
obtainable to sell the best of their young
stock, thus the breed steadily degenerated,
until the late Prince Consort sent a grey Arab
stallion to stand at New Park. The effects
of this fresh strain of blood were soon evident;
but history, as exemplified by the beneficial
results of Marske's service, repeated itself;
the commoners were too ready to sell the
pick of the young animals, whereby the benefits which should have accrued were heavily
discounted

It must be explained that the large breeders
have running in the Forest a hundred ponies,
or even more; many breeders possess forty
or fifty; while the small occupiers own as many
as they can keep during the winter. Their
sole responsibility to the Court of Verderers
in respect of the ponies is the "marking fee"
(raised in 1897 from eighteen pence to two
shillings per head), which goes to the Common
fund The marking system should enable the
Court to know how many ponies are running
in the Forest, and the census taken about
ten years ago showed about 3,000 animals,
of which it was estimated some 1,800 were
breeding mares.

At the present time it is estimated that the number does not exceed 2,500 head. Higher wages and more remunerative occupations tend to deter the younger generation from devoting their attention to pony breeding ; and as the old pony lovers pass away many droves of ponies are broken up and sold out of the forest

From spring to autumn the droves range the Forest at will, affecting, of course, the best pasturage, or, in the heat of summer, the shadiest localities , in winter some of the ponies are taken into pastures, the remaining animals being left at large.

It is to be observed that the most profitable animals are the hardy ones, which run in the Forest all the year round. The majority of the young animals are handled only for the purpose of marking, and are never, if possible, driven off their own ground Thus, unless strange stallions are used, it is very difficult to change the blood, the forest-born stallion remaining in his own locality and collecting his own harem around him " In-and-in " breeding was therefore inevitable before the New Forest Pony Association was established.

Besides these 2,500, it is estimated that about the Forest neighbourhood some 2,000 ponies are worked in light carts and other vehicles, and as many of these ponies are used for breeding purposes, it will be seen

what an important source of pony supply we
have in the New Forest district.

When the influence of the Arab sire sent
by the Prince Consort ceased to be felt,
degeneration again set in, the decreased
prices brought by ponies at the fairs proving
conclusively how the breed was deteriorating.
To combat the evil the Court of Verderers
in 1885 hired four well-bred stallions, which
were kept by the "Agisters," or marksmen,
for the service of commoners' mares at nominal
fees. Two seasons' experience proved that
the Court funds would not bear the strain,
and the horses were sold; with the less
hesitation because it was found that in the
absence of any inducement to the breeders
to retain promising young stock, good foals
and bad were alike sent for sale to the fairs
The wild mares, moreover, were not of course
covered by these stallions, and the majority
of the New Forest stock obtained no benefit
from their presence in the district.

The "ponies in hand," nevertheless, were
more than sufficiently numerous to be considered, and in 1889 it was arranged to
provide the necessary inducement to keep
promising youngsters by giving premiums at
a stallion show in April of each year, winners
of premiums to run in the Forest till the
following August; and this scheme has been

productive of very marked results in the way of keeping good stock to reproduce their kind.

Her late Majesty, in 1889, lent two Arab stallions, Abeyan and Yirassan, for use in the district, and these, remaining for two and three seasons respectively, did much good. A son of the former, out of a Welsh mare, now stands in the district. His owner, Mr. Moens, states that his produce show great improvement, and his services are in eager demand among the commoners   The general improvement in the Forest ponies since 1890 is very striking.*

Lack of funds has seriously handicapped the New Forest Pony Association in its work, and the burden of carrying out the programme has fallen upon the shoulders of a few   Conspicuous among those who have borne the

---

* Messrs. Robert Bradford and Frederick Tuck, who judged the ponies at the Association's Show of 1902, reported improvement in all the classes. So good were the forty-one exhibits in the class for ponies four years old and upwards that £1 premiums were awarded to the sixteen ponies which did not win one of the twenty-five £2 awards offered   The three-year-old class numbered twenty-four ponies against sixteen in the previous year, and showed much improvement. The two-year-old class was well filled and included some promising stock, but the exceptional merit of the yearling class proved how successful have been recent endeavours to improve the breed.

lion's share of the task is Lord Arthur
Cecil, who now turns out no fewer than
twenty-two stallions for the benefit of the
commoners generally. For many years past
Lord Arthur has interested himself in the
improvement of the breed, he has been
using with success stallions of a distinct and
hardy breed from the Island of Rum off the
West Coast of Scotland.

These are the Black Galloways which were
found in a wild state on the island in 1840,
by the late Marquis of Salisbury, and were
always kept pure. Lord Arthur secured the
whole stock in the year 1888. His interesting letter on the subject of the ponies, which
for the last ten years have been increasingly
used in the New Forest, is appended.

"The Rum ponies, which were much thought of
by my father, seem to be quite a type of themselves,
having characteristics which would almost enable one
to recognise them anywhere. Every one of those I
bought in 1888 had *hazel*, not *brown* eyes, and though
only a small boy in 1862, when six or seven of those
ponies came to Hatfield, I can remember that they
also had the hazel eye. They have, almost without
exception, very good hind-quarters, with the tail well
set up; and it is in this respect that I hope they will
do good in the New Forest On the other hand, they
have big plain heads which are not liked by the commoners This defect, however, is rapidly disappearing
with good keep, as it does with all breeds of ponies

"After I bought the ponies in 1888 and began
breeding, I was at a loss to know how to continue the
breed, as I could not well use the stallion which accom-

panied the mares to his own progeny. I remembered
having seen at the Highland and Agricultural Society's
Show, in 1883, a stallion which had interested me very
much, being exactly like the ponies I remembered
coming to Hatfield I enclose . . . . copy of a
letter* received from his breeder . . It is curious
that I should have thus dropped on to exactly the same
kind of thing that my father is supposed to have used,
he used the same blood years ago as the writer of the
letter.

" When my mother visited Rum the people of the
adjacent island of Canna gave her a pony mare which
I also remember, very old, at Hatfield. She was of
a rich cream colour, she threw a foal which had all
the characteristics, the hazel eye, long croup and big
head.

" I have noticed all the deer-stalking ponies I
could see on the look-out for some of these characteristics, but, with the exception of the hazel eye and
a somewhat strong inclination towards blackness in
colour, I cannot say that I have seen much trace of
the same kind of pony on the mainland in Scotland
This, however, is no doubt rather through crossing
with other strains than because they have not some
of the original blood, and I feel sure that the Galloway
of olden days was of the same type, though that term
has now come to mean something quite different and
in no way connected with the district on the West
Coast of Scotland

" The hazel eye is not uncommon on Exmoor, and
occurs in the Welsh pony. It would be a very interesting study to try and trace the tendency to show that
colour ; it would, I think, throw light on the ancestry
of many horses and ponies, or, at least, it would reveal
many curious instances of *reversion*."

---

* " The pony (Highland Laddie) . . . was bred
by us at Coulmour, Ross-shire; being the youngest, I
think, of seven foals thrown by the black mare, Polly,
to Allen Kingsburgh (Lord Lovat's stallion) . . .

Lord Arthur, in conclusion, deprecates the
susceptibility of pony breeders generally to the
influence of fashion ; he is of opinion that
efforts made in some districts to increase size,
while efforts elsewhere are directed to its
reduction, cannot in the long run be beneficial ,
whereas, if Nature were allowed to determine
the size of pony suitable for each locality,
valuable results might be obtained by crossing
the different breeds It is quite certain that
the perpetuation of a breed larger than the
character of the country and pasture can
support can only be secured by the constant
introduction of alien blood, which in course of
time will completely alter the local stamp, and
not necessarily for the better.

It may be noticed in this connection that
the suckers which are sold in large numbers
every season, and which are taken to Kent,
Surrey, Essex and elsewere, respond in marked
degree to the influence of good pasturage
They increase in height and in substance,
growing to from 13.2 to 14 hands.

The Hon. Gerald Lascelles, Deputy Sur-
veyor of the New forest, has said of this
locality :—

Most of her foals, if not all, were shown by us and
won prizes at country and the Highland Agricultural
Society's Meetings in the North. Her third foal, Glen,
a jet-black stallion, took 2nd prize in his class at the
Aberdeen Show in 1880 (I think) "

" You have a magnificent run for your ponies. Your
mares might breed from ponies of almost any quality
.   .   .   .   Ponies running out all winter in the
mountains of Ireland and of Wales, on Exmoor, in
Cornwall, and on the Cumberland and Yorkshire fells,
have a far worse climate to face than that of the New
Forest, and no better pasture   Such ponies would
laugh at the hardships of the New Forest. '

The New Forest pony is perhaps less hardy
than some of the hill breeds, but his constitution is quite robust enough to be one of his
most valuable attributes , and opinions are not
unnaturally divided as to the desirability of
increasing his size, if gain of inches means
sacrifice of hardiness   Thirteen hands was
the height the Forest breeders formerly
admitted to be the maximum desirable , but
of recent years their views on this point have
been somewhat enlarged.

The close resemblance of the Rum ponies to
the native of the New Forest marks out these
stallions as peculiarly suitable for crossing
purposes   For this reason, and also because
their number must exercise strong and speedy
influence upon the wild Forest mares, the
foregoing particulars have been given in detail.

Lord Arthur Cecil believes that the Welsh
pony stallion of about 13 1 or 13·2 would be
as good a cross for the New Forest pony as
any now obtainable.

Lord Ebrington, who bought Exmoor and the Simonsbath stud of improved Exmoor ponies, lent one of his stallions to the New Forest Association in the summer of 1898, and this sire has done good service among the wild mares, and still runs during the season in the Forest.

When broken the New Forest ponies are generally far more spirited than the ordinary run of British ponies. The practice of using the "ponies in hand" for driving the wild mobs to be branded, &c, teaches them to turn quickly and gallop collectedly on rough ground ; they thus acquire great cleverness.

As regards their market value, the following letter from Mr W. J. C. Moens, a most energetic member of the Council of the Association which he founded, gives the best idea.

"At the Ringwood Fair, December 11th, 1897, there was a larger outside demand for suckers than ever experienced, buyers coming from Kent, Sussex, Surrey, Essex, Somersetshire and Dorsetshire The prices ran from £4 to £6 10s., the larger dealers buying about fifty to sixty each, which they trucked (25 to 30 in a truck) away by rail One lot of about 55 of these foals, only recently taken from their dams, were sold at once by auction at Brighton, and realised £6, £7 and £8 each, one fetching £10 They improve enormously on good keep Our Forest feed is hardly good enough; on richer lands the ponies grow nearly a hand higher and get more substance Since our Association has improved the breed, of late years, very many have gone to the Kent Marshes, where they are highly thought of, very much more so than the Dartmoor ponies Yearlings at Lyndhurst Pony Fair, in August, fetched £5 to £8, but the average was spoiled by two large sales by auction of 'lane haunters'—old mares and other cast-offs—which realised small prices. . . . I have seen some of our improved ponies at Hastings and elsewhere, broken in, and about five years old. They are much valued and sell for about £25. . . The general improvement since 1889 or 1890 is very marked, and, though there was some opposition to the idea of bettering the 'real Forester' at first, now all admit the benefit of the work."

For the information of those interested in this breed, the following description, furnished to the Polo Pony Society for their Stud Book (vol v) by the New Forest Local Committee, may be quoted :—

"*For the New Forest pony it is difficult to give any exact description, but the best class of them are from 12 hands to 13 hands 2 inches high, according to the portion of the Forest on which they are reared. If taken off the Forest when they are weaned and well kept during the first two winters, they are said very often to attain the size of 14 hands 1 inch There is sometimes an apparent deficiency of bone, but what there is should be of the very best quality. The feet are wide and well formed. They are often considered goose rumped, but their hocks should be all that could be desired In colour they may be said to range through every variety, though there are not many duns, and few, if any, piebalds left. The flea-bitten greys which are still very numerous on the Forest show strong traces of an Arab cross The shoulders, though not always what might be desired in point of depth, are almost invariably fine and well laid It is a great characteristic of the New Forest pony to be always gay and alert, and, though they are extremely good-tempered and docile when fairly broken, they are quite indomitable until they are completely cornered The true Forester is never sulky.*"

WELSH PONIES.

At the period when Wales was an independent kingdom live stock was protected by a singularly comprehensive series of laws. These were originally codified by Howel Dda, a prince who reigned from A D. 942 to 948, and at a somewhat later period they were embodied in three distinct legal codes, the Venedotian, Dimetian and Gwentian, applicable respectively to North, South and South-eastern Wales, conforming to the local customs which prevailed in each area.

Under these laws no Welsh serf was permitted to sell a stallion without the permission of his lord The value of a horse (or, accurately speaking, pony, as the hill ponies were the only equine stock the country possessed in those days) was laid down without regard to individual merit till he reached his third year

A foal until a fortnight old was worth four pence ; from the fifteenth day of his age till one year old, 24 pence ; when a year and one day old he was worth 4S pence, and stood at that value till he began his third year, when he was valued at 60 pence.   When

in his third year he was broken in, and his
value depended on the work he was fitted for.
A palfrey or sumpter horse was valued at
120 pence, and a working horse to draw cart
or harrow 60 pence.

It was not permissible to use horses, mares
or cows for ploughing for fear of injury, oxen
only might be employed for such labour
Any entire male animal was worth three
females; thus a wild stallion was worth nine
score pence to the mare's value of three score
pence

If a horse were sold he was to be
warranted against staggers for three nights,
against "black strangles " * for three months,
and against farcy for a year. He was to
be warranted against restiveness until the
purchaser should have ridden him three times
"amid concourse of men and horses", and
if he proved restive the seller had to refund
one-third of the price he had received.

The value of each part of the horse was
strictly specified by these laws; the worth
of his foot was equal to his full value, each
eye was esteemed worth one-third of his full

---

* The commentators believe the disease so termed to
be glanders, but inasmuch as the warranty against
farcy held good for twelve months, perhaps we should
accept this reading with reserve.

value. For every blemish in a horse one-
third of the total worth was to be returned,
his ears and tail included : a not obscure hint
that cropping and docking were practised in
Wales at this period, and that opinions varied
concerning the desirability of the operations

That docking was in vogue is certain, for
a special clause makes the "tail of a filly for
common work" worth the total value of the
animal. The peculiar value of the tail of a
"filly for common work" lay in the fact that
the harrow was often secured to the tail, as
was the practice in parts of Ireland and Scotland until near the end of the eighteenth
century. Arthur Young refers to the practice.
When he visited the co Cavan, in 1776, he
found to his astonishment that the people
"very commonly plough and harrow with their
horses drawing by the tail." The people
insisted that when the horses were tired
from collar work all that was necessary to
rest them was to strip off their harness and
secure the plough or harrow to the tail.

In Wales, as in other parts of Britain, the
mare was preferably used for draught and pack
work, horses being reserved for military service. The mane and bridle were worth the
same amount, viz., four pence, the forelock
and halter were also coupled as worth one
penny each.

Howel Dda's "Law of Borrowing" was equally comprehensive. The man who borrowed a horse and fretted the hair on his back was to pay four pence; if he broke the skin to the flesh eight pence, and if skin and flesh were broken to the bone sixteen pence. Borrowing without the owner's leave was expensive: the borrower had to pay four pence for mounting, and four pence for each rhandir (supposed to be a league) he rode the horse He also had to pay a fine to the owner's lord.

If a hired horse fell lame or was injured by accident the owner had to furnish the hirer with one equally good until the injured horse recovered

The laws which regulated compensation for trespass show that it was customary to fetter or clog the horses when they were turned out to graze. Trespass by day in corn by a clogged horse was to be compensated by payment of one penny, and trespass by night twopence. Trespass by a horse free of restraint was recompensed by half those sums. In this connection it must be noted that stallions were "privileged", and though a broken-in entire ran at large for three seasons (seasons from mid April to mid May and the month of October), he did not lose the privilege which relieved his

owner from fine for any damage he might
do in the standing crops.

The Welsh pony is more numerous than
any other breed He wanders over the hills
and waste lands in all the twelve counties
of the Principality, and also on the borders
of Shropshire, Herefordshire and Monmouth ,
whereas his congeners are limited to areas
insignificant by comparison. The distribution
is, of course, very unequal, the strength and
number of droves varying with the character
of the country ; there are no statistics in
existence, nor has there been made any
estimate of the number of Welsh ponies.

Many of the common lands which were
once open to the Welsh pony have been
enclosed of recent years ; but in spite of his
exclusion from the better pastures and the
warfare waged against him by shepherds
and their dogs in the interests of grazing for
sheep, he thrives marvellously.

There are thousands of acres of wet and
boggy lands whose grasses "rot " sheep, but
which afford the hardy pony nourishing diet.
In some districts he is kept on the move
almost as unceasingly as are the deer in
Scotland or on Exmoor , and the life he
leads has done much to develop his instincts
of self-preservation

Accustomed from earliest foalhood to the

4

roughest ground, he is sure-footed as the
goat, and neither punishment nor persuasion
will induce him to venture upon unsafe bog.
He has good shoulders, strong back, neat
head and most enduring legs and feet, he is,
in short, a strong, sound and useful animal.
Some of the stoutest and best hunters bred
on the borders of Wales trace their descent
from the Welsh pony mare crossed with the
thoroughbred sire, and the same may be
said of some of the best modern steeple-
chasers.

J C Loudon, in his work, *An Encyclopædia of Agriculture*, published in 1825,
writes :—

"The Welsh horse bears a near resemblance in
point of size to the best native breed of the Highlands of Scotland. It is too small for the two-horse
ploughs, one that I rode for many years, which, to
the last, would have gone on a pavement by choice,
in preference to a softer road."

Again, the celebrated sporting writer,
"Nimrod" (C J. Apperley), in his book
The Horse and the Hound, published in
1842, writes of this breed as follows:—

"They are never lame in the feet, or become
roarers, they are also very little susceptible of
disease in comparison with other horses, and as a
proof also of their powers of crossing a country, the
fact may be stated of the late Sir Charles Turner
riding a pony ten miles in forty-seven minutes, and
taking thirty leaps in his course, for a wager of 1,000

guineas, with the late Duke of Queensberry. . .
The Earl of Oxford had a mare pony, got by the Clive
Arabian, her dam by the same horse, out of a Welsh
mare pony, which could beat any of his racers four miles
at a feather-weight, and during the drawing of the Irish
lottery the news was conveyed express from Holyhead
to London chiefly by ponies, at the rate of nearly twenty
miles an hour."

Endeavours have been made from time to
time to improve the breed, but these efforts
until quite recently were made by individuals,
and the benefits, when any followed, were
local and temporary. The first recorded introduction of superior alien blood occurred in
the first quarter of the eighteenth century,
when that famous little horse, Merlin, was
turned out to summer on the Welsh hills after
his retirement from the Turf. The small
horses which George II.'s Act (p. 8) sought
to banish from the racecourse were not all
worthless, " vile and paltry " they may have
been as a class, but there were some good
ones among them, and Merlin was the best
This little horse, who owed his name to the
smallest of British hawks, beat every animal
that started against him, and enjoyed a career
of uninterrupted success until he broke down ,
he was then purchased by a Welsh gentleman,
said to have been an ancestor of Sir Watkin
Williams Wynn, and turned out to run with
the droves on the hills. So remarkable was

the improvement wrought upon the breed by
this one stallion that in course of a few years
the value of the ponies in that locality greatly
increased. The name of the sire was applied
to his stock and their descendants, which
became famous as "Merlins"; and the
certificate that proved an animal one of the
true Merlin breed made all the difference in
the market.

That usually accurate authority, Richard
Berenger, in his *History and Art of Horsemanship*, says, the Welsh breed, "once so
abundant, is now [1771] nearly extinct"; but
in this he must have been mistaken, as there
is evidence from the district to show that
twenty-six years later it was very far from
extinct. "A farmer" writes to the *Gentleman's Magazine* of July, 1797, complaining
of the "injurious increase of the smallest
breed of ponies, which are no kind of use,"
and which, he says, do an immense amount of
mischief to the growing corn. He ventured
to assert that for one cow found trespassing
ten ponies would be seen, and strongly urged
that an Act of Parliament should be passed
forbidding right of common to horses under
14 hands high.

In the middle of the last century, when
fast-trotting animals for harness and saddle
were in great demand, it was thought desirable

to see what could be done with the Welsh
pony, and accordingly Comet, Fireaway,
Alonzo the Brave, and other fast-stepping
small-sized Hackney sires were brought from
Norfolk into Cardiganshire and Breconshire
to cross with the native ponies.

Such a cross could hardly fail to result in a
strong, fast-trotting and useful pony when we
consider that the Norfolk Hackney traces his
descent in a direct line to the Darley Arabian.
The Darley Arabian, foaled 1702, was the sire
of Flying Childers, foaled 1715, the speediest
racehorse, of his time, and was considered by
many a better horse than Eclipse.

The Report issued by the recent Royal
Commission on Land in Wales and Mon-
mouthshire contains some remarks on the
subject which must be reproduced here —

"With regard to cobs and ponies, breeding in this
direction is a much larger factor in the farming of
Wales   There is plenty of material to make use of,
and the breeding of ponies might be made much more
profitable than it is at present   In the counties of
Radnor and Brecon there has been some systematic
attempts to encourage the breeding of cobs, with
satisfactory results.   On the mountains of North
Wales, which were formerly famous for wild herds
of 'Merlins,' little has, however, been done   Lord
Penrhyn purchased an excellent stallion, Caradoc, who
might have done much good had he been more patron-
ised   The fault seems to lie in the careless treatment
of the herds of ponies, which are allowed to ramble at
will, winter and summer, to live or starve as Nature

may please No attention whatever is paid to the
breeding, the herds being wild to all intents and
purposes It seems a pity that such waste should be
allowed The stoutness and endurance of the Welsh
pony is proverbial, and if attention were paid to
selection in breeding, separation of the sexes, and
feeding and shelter in the winter, an exceedingly
valuable addition to the mountain farmer's profits might
be found at a small cost

"Turning to the evidence upon this subject Mr.
J. E Jones, who appeared before us at Tregaron, gave
it as his opinion that the breed of cobs was deteriorating while Mr. Bowen Woosnam, of Tynygrug, near
Builth, himself a successful breeder, stated that not
nearly as much attention was paid to breeding cobs as
formerly. Mr Woosnam also said If Welsh farmers
were to have a portion of their money invested in ponies
and cobs which are suitable to the farms that they are
occupying, they would derive proportionately a larger
income from them than they would from the cattle or
sheep that they are rearing.   . . I do not mean
to say that their stock should exclusively consist of
ponies and cobs, but that they should have a few on
every suitable farm There is the greatest difficulty at
the present time in getting good ponies and cobs."

The Commissioners were evidently unaware
of the work which has been done by the
Church Stretton Hill Pony Improvement
Society. This society was formed to encourage and assist the farmers in the work of
improving the ponies which they only too
generally neglect. The plan followed was to
take up the best of the native stallions for
service· those of the truest type only were
used, and the improvement in the young stock
got by these selected sires was marked : they

showed more compactness of build, better bone and greater spirit than their promiscuously-bred brethren of the wilds. There can be no doubt but that continuance of work on these lines would do much towards converting the scarcely saleable raw material of the Hills into profitable stock

Running more or less wild on the hills in the immediate neighbourhood of Church Stretton are ponies closely allied to and very similar to the Welsh mountain breed

The *Field* of September 28th, 1895, contains a spirited account of the work of "Rounding up the Longmynd Ponies," Longmynd being the name of the picturesque range of hills behind Church Stretton The object of the business is to collect the scattered droves belonging to various owners and deal with the ponies as their qualities may suggest. The driving, in which numerous mounted helpers take part, is rather in the nature of sport than labour, and affords ample opportunity for the exercise of horsemanship, since the mobs are very unwilling to leave their accustomed haunts, and display both cunning and obstinacy

"The last rebellion on the part of the ponies being quashed, the whole drove, numbering between 400 and 500, is bundled down a narrow lane and out on to the high road Finally they are driven *en masse* down the main street of Church Stretton, and are herded in a large yard in the centre of the town, where they are dealt with according to the will of their several owners. Many are sold, others branded, and the weedy yearlings are drawn out with a view of preventing any possible deterioration in the stock of the future This annual overhauling has done a very great deal towards maintaining the standard of merit of the breeding stock on the hill , and if properly worked, and the various owners continue to combine for the common good, the Longmynd ponies will soon become a valuable breed."

These ponies usually range from 10 hands to 11 hands 2 inches in height, 12 hands 2 inches being considered the outside limit. Mr. John Hill, of Marshbrook House, Church Stretton, in his endeavours to breed polo ponies, has shown that a valuable riding and harness animal can be obtained by judicious crossings on the Welsh pony About the year 1891 Mr Hill purchased several of the best and most typical mares, wild and unbroken, from the hills these mares, which averaged only 10 hands, were put to an Arab.

His stock were handsome, compact and hardy, and grew to an average height of 13 hands. The fillies of this cross when two years old were put to the best Welsh pony procurable, a 14 hands 1 inch stallion, with riding shoulders and showing bone and quality These mares were subsequently put to a small thoroughbred, and to him threw foals full of quality and in every way promising.

Mr. Hill's breeding experiments have all been made with the 14 hands 2 inch polo pony in view : and he has shown that Welsh ponies judiciously crossed with suitable alien blood produce stock for which a ready market should be found.

Mr. W. J. Roberts, the Hon. Secretary of the Church Stretton Hill Pony Society, states that he has tried the Arab cross, but "the offspring is useless on the hills " A half-bred Arab is not the animal to successfully withstand the hardships and exposure of half-wild existence on the Welsh hills. The object sought in improving the Welsh or any other of these breeds is not to fit it for a life of semi-wildness, but to make it more serviceable to man

The work of the Welsh Pony and Cob Society, founded in the year 1902, has been prosecuted with great success. The first volume of its Stud Book contains the names of 38 stallions and 571 mares and a provisional register of 29 stallions and 188 mares , while the members' roll numbers about 300 This Society divides the animals, whose breeding and improvement its aim is to encourage, into four divisions, viz :—

CLASS A —The pure Welsh pony type not exceeding 12 hands 2 inches.

CLASS B.—Ponies of from 12 hands 2 inches

to 13 hands 2 inches where a cob cross has been introduced direct from the Welsh pony.

CLASS C —Ponies of from 13 hands 2 inches to 14 hands 2 inches which have in their veins a stronger infusion of cob blood.

CLASS D —Welsh cobs of from 14 hands 2 inches to 15 hands 2 inches, which are the largest Welsh-bred animals used in the Principality

Nearly all the cob and pony breeders of Wales are represented on the list of members, and it cannot be doubted that this well-organised endeavour to discriminate between the classes of animal bred on the hills, and improve each by recognised standards of merit, must be productive of excellent results

For information of those interested in this breed the following descriptions, furnished to the Polo Pony Society for their Stud Book (vol. v.) by the Local Committees, may be quoted :—

(NORTH WALES DIVISION)

HEIGHT *Not to exceed 12 hands 2 inches* COLOUR *Bay or brown preferred , grey or black allowable , but dun, chestnut, or broken colour considered objectionable* ACTION *Best described as that of the hunter, low " daisy-cutting " action to be avoided. The pony should move quickly and actively, stepping out well from the shoulder, at the same time flexing the hocks and bringing the hind legs well under the body when going* GENERAL CHARACTER. *The pony should show good " pony " character and evidence of robust constitution, with* the unmistakable appearance of hardiness peculiar to mountain ponies, and at the same time have a lively appearance   HEAD   Should be small, well chiselled in its outline and well set on; forehead broad, tapering towards nose   NOSTRILS.   Large and expanding.   EYES   Bright, mild, intelligent and prominent   EARS.   Neatly set, well formed and small. THROAT AND JAWS   Fine, showing no signs of coarseness or throatiness   NECK   Of proportionate length, strong but not too heavy, with a moderate crest in the case of the stallion. SHOULDERS.   Good shoulders most important, should be well laid back and sloping, but not too fine at the withers nor loaded at the points.   The pony should have a good long shoulder-blade   BACK AND LOINS.   Strong and well covered with muscle   HIND-QUARTERS.   Long, and tail well carried, as much like the Arab as possible, springing well from the top of back.   HOCKS.   Well let down, clean cut, with plenty of bone below the joint.   They should not be "sickled" or "cow-hocked"   FORE-LEGS.   Well placed, not tied in any way at the elbows, good muscular arm, short from the knee to the fetlock joints, flat bone, pasterns sloping but not too long, feet well developed and open at the heel, hoof sound and hard.

(SOUTH WALES DIVISION)

The South Wales hill pony seldom exceeds 13 hands, and in a pure state is about 12 hands   His attributes are a quick, straight action and sure-footedness, he is low in the withers, short in his forehand, and with faulty hind-quarters as far as appearance goes, his tail being set on low and his hocks sickled, but his forelegs and feet are good.   His head and eyes show breed, courage and sense, and his constitution is strong or he could not live where he does.   Of late years he has been crossed with the Cardiganshire cob to some extent; and half-bred two-year-old shire colts have been allowed access to the hills in summer in some places, much to the detriment of the breed.   In colour, bays and brown prevail

EXMOOR AND DARTMOOR PONIES.

It is certain that ponies have run in these districts for many centuries in a practically wild state, and probably have always supplied the tillers of the soil with beasts of burden. In times when these localities were without roads of any kind, and wheeled traffic was impossible, the sled and the pack-horse were used for transporting agricultural produce.

The sleds were drawn by oxen and small horses, and the ponies were employed to carry corn, &c., in pots and panniers, the ponies used for this purpose being selected from the animals which ran at large upon the wastes.

Fifty years ago and less, pack-horses might be met with in the western and southern districts. They were the larger ponies of the Dartmoor and Exmoor breed, and were indispensable to the farmers whose holdings at that time lay beyond the region of roads in secluded districts

The practice of taking up a few of the best mares for breeding purposes and keeping them in enclosed pasture is no doubt an old one, but the vast majority of the droves have always been left to their own devices They bred and interbred without let or hindrance, and by consequence the weakly died off, leaving the fittest, *i e.*, the hardiest and the best able, to withstand the rigours of exposure

Carew, in his *History of Cornwall*, which was written in the early part of the reign of James I. (1603-1625), says :—

"The Cornish horses are hardly bred, coarsely fed, and so low in stature that they were liable to be seized on as unstatutable, according to the statute of Henry VIII., by anyone who caught them depasturing the commons "

In the year 1812, Exmoor was disforested by George III , and a commission was appointed to survey and value the lands. The total acreage was found to be 18,810 acres, of which 10,262 acres were adjudged the property of the Crown. In 1820, Mr. John Knight purchased the Crown allotment , at a later date he acquired Sir Thomas Acland's portion, and Sir Arthur Chichester's property of Brendon which adjoined it, the total area so acquired being over 16,000 acres.

Sir Thomas Acland had bred ponies, and when Mr. Knight bought the land he applied himself to the task of improving the ponies, which for some years previously had been fetching only from £4 to £6. The low prices

obtainable, we infer, were due in a measure
to the ease with which the local shepherds
"took liberal tithe" of the ponies, which,
despite the anchor-brand they bore to prove
ownership, were readily purchased in Wiltshire

Ponies were to be had at an even lower price
at the time referred to. Mr C. P Collyns,
in his work, *The Chase of the Wild Red
Deer*, says that in the year 1816 he "bought
an Exmoor pony for 23s (a fair price in those
days) at Simonsbath. When haltered, that is,
caught and secured for the first time in his
life, he proved to be two years old   .
the pony was only 11 hands high." It may
be added that Mr. Collyns' nephews and nieces,
to the number of nine, learned to ride on this
pony, and when twenty years old, it carried a
man to hounds "in such a manner as to excite
his surprise and the envy of many a sportsman apparently better mounted"

The only pure Exmoor ponies now existing, so far as enquiry has disclosed, are those
bred by Sir T Dyke Acland, Bart., of Holni-
cote, Taunton   When Sir Thomas Acland
sold his Exmoor property to Mr. Knight
he removed his original uncrossed stock to
Winsford Hill, near Dulverton ; these ponies
alone preserve the full characteristics of the
old strain , they run from 11 hands 2 inches
to 12 hands 2 inches, are dark brown with

black points, and have the mealy tan muzzle. It is stated that only about a dozen mares were left in their old quarters

Mr Knight and some other gentlemen were attracted by the accounts of the Dongola Arab horses given by the great traveller Bruce, and after considerable delay a number of stallions and mares were procured through the British Consul in Egypt. They proved to be black, short-backed animals with lean heads and rather Roman noses Their hind-quarters were good, but, unlike the typical Arab, they had "flattish ribs" Mr. Knight became the owner of two sires and three mares, which he brought to Simonsbath. One of these Dongola stallions was mated with a number of 12 hands Exmoor mares ; the foals generally grew to about 14 hands 2 inches, and though they followed their dams in the colour of coat, the distinctive mealy muzzle disappeared. There was a de-sire to retain as much of the Exmoor character as was compatible with improvement in the breed , hence those half-bred mares by the Dongola horse which did not retain as much as possible of the native type were drafted from the stud.

A small thoroughbred horse, "Pandarus," standing under 15 hands, son of Whalebone, succeeded the Dongola horse , foals of his get

retained the original colour but were smaller,
ranging from 13 hands to 13 hands 2 inches.
Another small thoroughbred, " Canopus," a
grandson of " Velocipede," followed " Pandarus " at the stud, and with equally satisfactory
results in respect of improved size and conformation ; but, as might have been expected,
these cross-bred ponies proved incapable of
enduring the hardships of moorland life when
turned out Hence, about 1844, Mr. Knight
gave up the use of alien blood and used his
own stallion ponies , the only exceptions being
Hero, a sturdy chestnut out of a Pandarus
mare, and Lillias, a grey of nearly pure Acland
strain.

After Mr. Knight's death, which event
occurred in 1850, the practice of selling the
ponies by private contact was abandoned in
favour of an annual auction, held at Simonsbath The comparative inaccessibility of the
spot, however, soon indicated the need of
change, and in 1854 the sale was first held at
Bampton Fair , and at a later date a batch of
broken ponies appears to have been sent
annually for sale by auction at Reading.

The system on which the ponies were kept
was also changed in the latter fifties , some
130 acres of pasture were set apart, and on
this the foals were wintered instead of remaining at large on the bleak hill-sides. The effect

thus produced upon the size and development of the young stock was very marked.

It 1863 the ponies mustered about four hundred strong, nearly one hundred of which were brood mares, young and old. In the *Sporting Magazine* of that year may be found a very full account of the Reading sale, which took place on September 30th.

" Seeing that Mr. Knight's half hundred Exmoor ponies walked in their neat and blue trimmed halters 140 miles ' direct from the hills' to Reading, the least we could do was to go and meet them there. The lot were bigger and better looking than they were in '61, when we were last there, nearer 13 hands and very much better broken.

" Three men are now constantly at them, both riding and driving all the year through, and the purchasers are no longer in a dire state of perplexity as to how they are to coax them home by fair means or foul

" Their journey occupies nine days to Reading, three of which are spent in a good grass field as an interlude.

. Prices have gone up steadily in three years to £13 19s 6d. which is £1 7s 6d. more than they made last year and fully three guineas beyond the average of '61. There were 32 bays (four of them 'buffy' and two of them ' rusty '), two chestnuts, both rather dark; three blacks, four browns, and nine (not very dappled) greys and venerable whites. The colours do not follow those of their great prototypes 'Marquis' and ' Dundee' were both bays certainly, and 'Hero' a chestnut, but ' Kettledrum' was a bay also, and ' Ranger' and ' Rifleman' iron greys. Such trifling varieties are not cared for on Exmoor.

" The top price this year was 34 guineas, and it was hardly to be expected that three such grand ex-sires could be found as 'The Sparcombe Pony,' Pandarus and Palmerston, which averaged 37 guineas the last

time they were sold. The ages varied between three
off and twelve off and the great bulk of them were
marked on the hoof with N, which signifies foaled in
1859. Seventy mare ponies have been put to this year,
and sons of the above crack trio (two of which won at
Barnstaple) have been used. The foals by a 14 hands
1 inch son of Old Port (the first-born of Beeswing) from
Devonshire pack mare are so promising that Mr. Knight
intends to have him back next season from the tenant
to whom he lent him."

The Mr. Knight referred to was no doubt
the heir of the gentleman who died in 1850,
and who did so much to improve the Exmoor
breed.

Much of the land which in former days was
given up to the droves has been reclaimed
during recent years, and improved methods of
cultivation have made it capable of growing
various crops and of grazing cattle and sheep.

Mr. Robert Smith, of Emmett's Grange,
also devoted attention to the improvement of
the Exmoor breed. Mr. Henry Hall Dixon,
"The Druid," who described a visit to Devonshire about the year 1860 or 1861, remarks
that "the original colour of the Exmoor seems
to have been a buffy bay, with a mealy nose,
and it is supposed to have preserved its character ever since the Phœnicians brought it over
when they visited the shores of Cornwall to
trade in tin and metals" Enquiry into the
ground for supposing that the original stock

was introduced by the Phœnicians would
perhaps produce results hardly commensurate
with the labour of research.

When the visit of "The Druid" was paid
only 250 acres of moorland remained unen-
closed, and the breeding stock on Mr. Smith's
holding consisted of "some twenty-five short-
legged brood mares of about 13 hands 2
inches." These passed the better part of the
year on the hills and were wintered in the
paddocks furnished with open sheds for shelter.

After experimenting with thoroughbreds,
Mr Smith procured a 14 hands pony, sire
named Bobby, by Round Robin out of an
Arab mare, and used him with the most en-
couraging results for two seasons Bobby's
stock were almost invariably bays. At a sale
held at Bristol, in 1864, twenty-nine cobs,
galloways and ponies, nearly all of which were
Bobby's get, made an average price of 23
guineas a head, several realising over 30
guineas. The highest price (figure not recorded) was paid for a bay stallion, five years
old and 13 hands high.

Whether Youatt refers to the improved
breed or not it is impossible to say, but that
authority states that about the year 1860 a
farmer who weighed 14 stone rode an Exmoor
pony from Bristol to South Molton, a distance
of 86 miles, beating the coach which travelled

the same road. This feat proves the pony to have been both fast and enduring.

A most competent authority who a couple of years ago paid a visit to Simonsbath to inspect the ponies of the district, describes the " Acland " as a wonderfully thoroughbred-looking and handsome pony with fine lean head, intelligent eye and good limbs The only fault he had to find was in the matter of size : he considered it a shade too small for general purposes.

The " Knights " were described as larger than the " Aclands " : they also retain the thoroughbred look derived from the Arab and other alien blood introduced by Mr. Knight in the second quarter of the century.

My informant remarks that one of the most interesting sights he witnessed was the display of jealousy by the stallions when two droves of ponies were brought up for inspection Each kept his harem crowded together apart from the other, " rounding in " his mares with the greatest fire, keeping at a far distance, in the hills, the weaker sires who might be suspected of designs upon the drove. Needless to say the little champion will show at his very best under such conditions

Among the gentlemen who have endeavoured to improve the Exmoor pony, mention must also be made of the Earl of

Carnarvon, Viscount Ebrington, and Mr.
Nicholas Snow, of Oare, who have breeding studs, but their strains, like those of the
farmers who rear a few each, are larger than
the representative "Aclands."

Dr Herbert Watney, of Buckhold, near
Pangbourne, until recently possessed herds
of Exmoor and Arab-Exmoor ponies; their
numbers have quite lately been greatly reduced by the sale of mares and young stock,
Dr. Watney holding the writer's view that
ground in time becomes staled if grazed by
numerous horses.* Dr. Watney laid the
foundations of his herd by the purchase of
about a dozen mares of the Knight and
Acland strains, and to serve them he
acquired the 13 hands 2 inch Exmoor stallion,
Katerfelto, winner of the first prize for pony
stallions at the Devon County Show, and
first prize in his class at the "Royal" in 1890.

The stallion runs with the mares, and the
herd lead on the Berkshire downs exactly the
same free life they led on Exmoor; they are
never brought under cover, and only when
snow buries the herbage in severe winters do
they receive a daily ration of hay. The richer
grazing and their exclusive service by Kater-

---

* See *Young Racehorses* (Suggestions for Rearing), by
Sir Walter Gilbey, Bart Vinton and Co., Ltd.

felto has resulted in distinct increase of size, the ponies ranging from 11 hands 3 inches to 13 hands 3 inches in height, yet retaining all the characteristics of the Exmoor native stock.

Dr Watney drafted off a number of the best mares to form a herd for service by the Arab pony stallion, Nejram, a bay standing 14 hands 1 inch, bred by Mr. Wilfred Blunt at Crabbet Park. Nejram's stock show in marked degree the distinctive character of their sire in the high set and carriage of the tail, full barrel, blood-like head and the long pastern, but at the same time they inherit from their dams the wonderful sure-footedness of the Exmoor pony. These ponies run from about 13 hands to 13 hands 3 inches. Half-a-dozen of these Arab-Exmoors, three years old, handled but unbroken, were sold in the year 1898 at an average price of over £14 14s. each. Twelve pure Exmoors, by Katerfelto, also handled but unbroken, three years old, brought an average of over £16 16s.

There is no doubt that at Dr. Watney's sale many of the animals were sold very cheaply; but he is entitled to congratulation on the success of his experiment, though it may not have proved remunerative. Nor can it be regarded as representative of the pony breeding industry, for we must bear in mind

that there is a wide difference between the
value of land in Berkshire and the value
of the wastes which form the home of the
Exmoor pony.

Bampton Fair, held in October, is now the
great rendezvous for Exmoor ponies Every
fair brings several hundred animals in from the
moors for sale, and good prices are obtained
under the hammer. They are much used for
small carriages and as children's ponies, and
some few may make polo ponies ; the less
desirable find ready sale to costermongers and
hawkers Newly-weaned suckers of five or
six months old fetch from £3 to £6 ; exceptionally promising youngsters command a
higher figure.

The Dartmoor pony's good points are a
strong back and loin, and substance. For
generations past the farmers appear to have
been in the habit of taking up a few mares for
riding and breeding purposes , to these diminutive dams a small Welsh cart stallion is put,
and the result is an animal hardy and serviceable enough for ordinary farm work. These
form a small minority.

For the most part the Dartmoor ponies still
run wild, shaggy and unkempt on the waste
lands on which they breed uncontrolled, on
which they are foaled and live and die ; often
without having looked through a bridle

Those taken up for riding purposes or for
breeding are of course the pick of the droves,
and thus we find an active force at work which
is calculated to lower the average standard of
quality among the wild ponies

In considering the various efforts which from
time to time have been made in the direction
of improvement by the introduction of fresh
blood, we must bear in mind that the mares
on which such experiments have been made
are those which have been taken up by farmers
and kept within fences.

We cannot find that stallions of alien blood
have ever been turned out to run on the moors,
and in view of the conditions under which the
moor ponies exist it is highly improbable that
such a stallion as would produce beneficial
results on the native breed would long enough
survive the exposure and scanty food to make
any appreciable mark thereon. Mares got by
crossing the Exmoor and Dartmoor strains
have been put to small blood horses with good
results.

Early in the present century Mr. Willing,
of Torpeak, made successful experiments in
crossing the Exmoor pony with the smaller
variety peculiar to the Dartmoor " tors " Mr.
Wooton, of Woodlands, says a writer in the
Field of October 9th, 1880, was in the habit
of purchasing mares of this cross from Mr.

Willing from about the year 1820, and possessed a considerable number of them. He used to put these to small racehorses standing in the district

The names of these thoroughbreds, Trap, Tim Whiffler, Rover, and Glen Stuart, are mentioned ; and about 1860 Mr. Wooton sent some of his Exmoor-Dartmoor mares to a small Arab belonging to Mr Stewart Hawkins, of Ivybridge. Mr. Wooton's endeavours to improve the Dartmoor breed are the first that were made on any considerable scale, so far as it is possible to discover.

About 1879 a resident who devoted much attention to the improvement of the Dartmoor breed introduced a brown stallion by Mr Christopher Wilson's Sir George out of Windsor Soarer, and as his mares—a selected lot, 12 hands 2 inches to 13 hands, either brown or chestnut—came in use, put them to this pony with the object of getting early foals. The young stock thus got were carefully weeded out, the best stallions and mares only being retained. The colt foals were kept apart and at two years old put to the mares got by their sire The experiment was very successful, browns, black - browns and chestnuts being the colours of this improved breed, which sold well

Mr. S. Lang, of Bristol, some years prior to

1884 sent for use in the district, Hereford, a
very small thoroughbred pony.

A description of Exmoor and Dartmoor
ponies exhibited at the Newton Abbot
Agricultural Show in May, 1875, may have
had reference to these improved ponies. The
following is quoted from the *Field* of May
29th in that year —

"Instead of deteriorating the stock improves yearly,
and the care which is now taken to infuse pure blood
without harming the essential characteristics of the
original denizen of the moor has succeeded in producing
an animal of superlative merit, fitted for any kind of
work, whether for the field, the road, or the collar. It
must be observed that the word 'moor' should apply
to Exmoor and the Bodmin wastes as well as the Forest
of Dartmoor, Dartmoor Forest itself being within the
precincts of the Duchy of Cornwall. The moor pony
or galloway of 14 hands is often in reality a little horse,
and when it is stated that Tom Thumb, the well-known
hunter of Mr Trelawny, was a direct descendant of the
celebrated Rough Tor pony of Landue, and that Foster
by Gainsborough, belonging to the late Mr. Phillips,
of Landue, carrying for many years fifteen stone and
upwards, was from a moor pony near Ivybridge, the
assertion is not made without bringing strong collateral
proof of the validity of the statement. Moreover, a
host of other examples could be added These animals
possess many of the properties of the thorough-bred—
speed, activity, any amount of stay, with legs of steel;
they can jump as well as the moor sheep, and much
after the same fashion, for no hedge fence can stop
either one or the other."

For the information of those interested in
this breed the following descriptions furnished

to the Polo Pony Society for their Stud Book
(vol. v.) by Local Committees may be quoted :—

(THL EXMOOR DIVISION.)

*The Exmoor pony should average 12 hands and never be
above 13 hands , moorland bred , generally dark bay or brown
with black points, wide forehead and nostril ; mealy nose ;
sharp ears ; good shoulders and back , short legs, with good
bone and fair action.*

*There are a few grey ponies in Sir Thomas Acland's herd,
but no chestnuts.*

(THE DARTMOOR DIVISION.)

The official description of points is identical
with that given for North Wales pony, with
certain amendments and additions :—

With regard to the height prescribed, " 14
hands for stallions and 13 hands 2 inches
for mares," the writer is assured by a gentleman whose knowledge of Dartmoor and
Dartmoor ponies is unquestioned, that it is
an error to lay down 14 hands as the
maximum height, a 13-hand pony being the
largest known.

HEIGHT *Not exceeding 14 hands for stallions, 13 hands
2 inches for mares* COLOUR. *Brown, black, or bay preferred , grey allowed, other colours objectionable* HEAD.
Should be small, well set on, and blood-like. NECK *Strong
but not too heavy, and neither long nor short , and, in case of
a stallion, with moderate crest.* BACK, LOINS, AND HIND
QUARTERS. *Strong and well covered with muscle.*

CUMBERLAND
AND WESTMORLAND PONIES

The ponies and galloways, for which the
waste lands of these counties have long been
known, appear to possess no distinguishing
characteristics that would permit it to be said
they form a distinct breed.   An authority
resident at Harrington who gives much information concerning the ponies of the "heafs"—
fell-side holdings—and moors, states that there
are several strains, and the appearance and
character of each differs in various districts
under the varying local influences of climate,
feed, &c.   Little or nothing is known of the
origin of these ponies.

The resemblance to "Shelties," borne by
those of certain localities until about the middle
of the century, suggested that they were descended from a mixed stock of galloways and
Shetland ponies , but some forty or fifty years
ago endeavours were made to improve them
by careful selection and mating; and the
resemblance, which did not necessarily imply
possession of the merits of the Shetland pony,
has in great measure disappeared.

They are generally good-tempered; so sure-footed that they can gallop down the steep hill-sides with surprising speed and fearlessness Their endurance has been remarked by many writers. Brown's *Anecdotes and Sketches of the Horse,* published about sixty years ago, contains an account of an extraordinary performance by a galloway, at Carlisle, in 1701, when Mr. Sinclair, of Kirkby Lonsdale, for a wager of 500 guineas, rode the animal 1000 miles in 1000 hours.

The stony nature of the heaf-lands requires only a light plough, which is easily drawn by one or two of the half-pony, half-horse nondescripts, the extent of arable land farmed by any one farmer is only from four to six acres.

A stallion is sometimes used for farm-work, and in such cases the neighbouring farmers bring mares to be served, some such stallions will serve from thirty to fifty mares in the season In the larger gangs running on the hill-sides, when more than one stallion is turned out, the fittest and strongest will select his harem and guard the mares with the greatest strictness.

In some cases a few ponies are taken up, broken and worked all the year round, carrying the farmer to market, drawing peat and hay, and ploughing. A good breeding mare often lives and dies without knowing a halter, running practically wild from the day she is dropped on the fell-side till she dies. These unhandled ponies pick up their living on the hills, and during winter a little hay is brought out to them by the shepherds.

The " Fell-siders," as the holders of heafs* are called locally, make no attempt to improve their wild pony stock ; under the existing conditions the wild mares drop their foals, it may be without. the knowledge of their owner. Farmers who bring their mares to a neighbour's working stallion exercise no discrimination in their choice , the cheapest and most accessible horse receives their preference.

Where skill and judgment have been brought to bear upon the improvement of the Fell ponies the result has been very marked. Mr. Christopher W. Wilson, of Rigmaden Park, Kirkby Lonsdale, Westmorland, was the pioneer of an improved breed of ponies, and he has shown what can be done with the material at hand, having built upon that foundation a breed which at the present day stands unrivalled for shape and action.

Having in the year 1872 taken the matter in hand, Mr. Wilson selected his breeding mares from among the best ponies of the districts, and put them to the pony stallion,

---

* Common rights holders

Sir George, who won eight first prizes at the
shows of the Royal Agricultural Society.

Sir George was by Sportsman (796), a brown
stallion, bred in Yorkshire and descended,
through Phenomenon,* a Norfolk Hackney,
in a direct line to Flying Childers, the speediest
racehorse of his time.

The female offspring from the selected mares
and Sir George were in due time mated with
their sire, and threw foals which showed
elegant and true Hackney characteristics in
far more marked degree than did their dams,
as might be anticipated in animals three-parts
instead of one-half bred.

The chief difficulty Mr Wilson had to con-
tend against was the tendency of these ponies
to exceed the 14 hands which was the limit of
the pony classes at all shows until the Royal
Show at Windsor in 1889.

Their height was kept down to the required
limit by turning out the young stock after the
first winter upon the rabbit warrens and moorlands of Rigmaden to find their own grazing
among the sheep and rabbits as their maternal
ancestors had done. This system not only
succeeded in its direct object, but went far to
preserve that hardiness of constitution which is

* *The Harness Horse*, by Sir Walter Gilbey, Bart.
Published in 1898, by Vinton and Co., Ltd., London.

by no means the least valuable attribute of the
mountain pony.

This judicious system of breeding and
management was maintained with the best
results ; the third direct cross from Sir George
produced a mare in Georgina V which had
constitution and stamina, and also more bone
than her dam or grand-dam.

The breeder's name has been given to the
fruits of his wisely directed efforts, and the
" Wilson pony " is now universally famous as
a trapper, for its shape and action, and for the
numerous successes it has achieved at the
principal shows at home and abroad

Mr. Wilson won the Queen's Jubilee gold
medals for both stallions and mares at the
Royal Agricultural Society's Show at Windsor,
in 1879, and sold the stallion for a large sum
to go to America On one occasion the Royal
Agricultural Society's Show included three
classes for pony stallions and three prizes in
each. Mr. Wilson entered nine ponies and
won all the nine prizes , also 1st and 2nd prizes
for pony brood mares

Sir Humphrey de Trafford, Bart., was also
most successful in producing ponies from stock
purchased from Mr. Christopher Wilson. At
the Flordon Sale, Norfolk, held in September,
1895, Sir Humphrey disposed of his large stud,
when some of the ponies realised prices which

are worth quoting . Snorer II., a brown mare,
13 hands 3 inches, eight years old, by Sir
George, dam Snorer by Sir George, 600
gs.: Georgina V, a bay mare, 14 hands, six
years old, by Sir George, dam Georgina II.,
by Sir George—Georgina, grand-dam also
by Sir George, 700 gs ; Dorothy Derby, a
bay mare, 14 hands, eight years old, by Lord
Derby II.—Burton Agnes, 600 gs , Dorothy
Derby II , a bay mare, 14 hands, six years
old, by Little Wonder II —Dorothy Derby,
720 gs. , Snorter II., bay filly, two years old,
by Cassius—Snorer II., by Sir George—
Snorer—Sir George, 700 gs. ; and Miss Sniff,
bay yearling filly, by Cassius—Snorer II.,
900 gs. ; the average for these six lots being
no less than £756

It is true that Sir Humphrey had spared
neither money nor labour in founding the
Flordon stud, and the ponies were animals of
exceptional merit. Their high quality had
won them prizes at all the principal shows in
England, and their fame was literally "world-
wide."

Over twenty years ago, the late Rev. J. M.
Lowther, rector of Boltongate, made an
attempt on a modest scale to improve the
ponies of the Caldbeck Fells by selecting sires
and dams from among the best of them Two
or three ponies of his breeding won prizes at

6

Whitehaven and Carlisle; his best sire was a
13 hands pony named Mountain Hero This
little animal had splendid bone and was as
hardy as the wildest of his kin. The picture
here given is a portrait of LITTLE WONDER
II, the property of the Marquis of Londonderry He was bred by Mr Christopher W.
Wilson, his sire being Little Wonder I., and
his dam Snorer by Sir George

Mr. William Graham, of Eden Grove,
Kirkbythorpe, Penrith, writes —

"Up to about twenty years ago great interest seems
to have been taken in pony or galloway cob breeding
throughout the whole district of the Eden valley in the
villages and hamlets that lie scattered all along the foot
of the Pennine range of hills. Previous to the days of
railway transit the ponies and small galloway cobs were
employed in droves as pack-horses, as well as for riding,
and many men now living can remember droves of from
twenty to thirty continually travelling the district,
carrying panniers of coal and other merchandise between
the mines and villages

"The village of Dufton, in which the hill farm of
Keisley is situated, was quite a centre of pony breeding,
and for many generations the Fell-side farmers in this
district have been noted for their ponies, they bred
them to the best Fell pony stallions, most of which were
trained trotters of great speed. Each of the three mares
originally purchased to found the stud at Keisley were
got from well-known locally-bred dams and grand-dams,
and all were selected to match each other in character
and style The mare from which two of them were
bred was from a very old strain by a stallion pony
called Ling * Cropper, a record trotter, and all the

* Ling being the local term for heather.

LITTLE WONDER II.

S. Clark, Hallgarth, Photo.

three mares were themselves by a pony called Blooming Heather, another well-known pony stallion of a few generations younger "

The Cumberland " Fell-siders " are wedded to the customs and usages of their ancestors, and endeavours to promote schemes for the general improvement of the ponies have met with small success. There certainly seems to be a very fair field in the district for breeding ponies, as they are very cheaply and easily reared, and when fit to break in can be disposed of for a very fairly good figure.

Colonel Green-Thompson, of Bridekirk, Cockermouth, in 1897, offered the farmers the opportunity of using an Arab stallion, but the chance of thus bettering their stock appears to have been neglected by the breeders This is to be regretted, for the fells and dales offer thousands of acres of good, sound grazing land which might be far more profitably devoted to pony-breeding than given up to the few scattered flocks of Herdwick sheep which they now carry.

The sheep farmers of Caldbeck and Matterdale in Cumberland pay some attention to the business, asserting that the ponies are less trouble and involve less risk than sheep Their fillies are put to the horse at two years old, and they frequently obtain a second foal before sending the dam to market. The colts command a readier sale than the mares. The ordinary Fell pony, outside the district, is in demand for pit work, for which purpose suitable animals bring from £12 to £15.

Mr. W. W. Wingate-Saul supplies the following description of the Fell ponies.—

"*A very powerful and compact cobby build, the majority having a strong middle piece with deep chest and strong loin characteristics, which, combined with deep sloping shoulders and fine withers, make them essentially weight-carrying riding ponies. The prevailing—indeed, the only—colours are black, brown, bay, and, quite occasionally, grey I do not remember ever having seen a chestnut, and if I found one I should think it due to the introduction of other blood. The four colours prevail in the order named, the best animals often being jet black and usually without white markings, unless it be a small white star. The head is pony-like and intelligent, with large bright eyes and well-placed ears. The neck in the best examples being long enough to give a good rein to the rider The hind-quarters are square and strong, with a well-set on tail. The legs have more bone than those of any of our breeds, ponies under 14 hands often measuring 8½ inches below the knee. Their muscularity of arm, thigh and second thigh is marvellous Their habitat (having been bred for centuries on the cold, inhospitable Fells, where they are still to be found) has caused a wonderful growth of hair, the winter coat being heavy and the legs growing a good deal of fine hair, all of which, excepting some at the point of the heel, is cast in summer Constitutionally they are hard as iron, with good all-round action, and are very fast and enduring.*"

IRELAND—THE CONNEMARA PONIES.

Richard Berenger, Gentleman of the Horse to King George III., in his work, *The History and Art of Horsemanship*, 1771, says that—

"Ireland has for many centuries boasted a race of horses called Hobbies, valued for their easy paces and other pleasing and agreeable qualities, of a middling size, strong, nimble, well moulded and hardy. . . . The nobility have stallions of great reputation belonging to them, but choose to breed for the *Turf* in preference to other purposes; for which, perhaps, their country is not so well qualified, from the moisture of the atmosphere, and other causes, which hinder it from improving that elastic force and clearness of wind, and which are solely the gifts of a dry soil, and an air more pure and refined This country, nevertheless, is capable of producing fine and noble horses."

The great stud maintained in England by Edward III. (1327-1377) included a number of Hobbies which were procured from Ireland. A French chronicler named Creton, who wrote a *Metrical History of the Deposition of Richard II*,* refers with great admiration to the Irish horses of the period. He evidently

---

* See vol. xx. of *Archeologia* for prose translation.

accompanied King Richard during his expedition to Ireland in the summer of 1399, for he says the horses of that country "scour the hills and vallies fleeter than deer"; and he states that the horse ridden by Macmore, an Irish chieftain, "without housing or saddle was worth 400 cows."

At a much later date the character of this breed was changed by the introduction of Spanish blood. Tradition asserts that the ponies which inhabited the rough and mountainous tracts of Connemara, in the county Galway, were descended from several animals that were saved from the wreck of some ship of the Spanish Armada in 1588.

It is, however, quite needless to invoke the aid of a somewhat too frequently employed tradition to explain the character which at one period distinguished these ponies. Spanish stallions were freely imported into England from the fourteenth to the seventeenth centuries; and it is probable that the character of the Connemara pony was derived not from shipwrecked stock but in more prosaic fashion by importation of sires from England.

The testimony of many old writers goes to prove the high esteem in which Spanish horses were held. The Duke of Newcastle, in his famous work on Horses and Horsemanship, written in 1658, says: " I have had

Spanish horses in my own possession which
were proper to be painted after, or fit for a
king to mount on a public occasion   Genets
have a fine lofty air, trot and gallop well.
The best breed is in Andalusia, especially
that of the King of Spain at Cordova."

The Spanish horses of those times owed
much to the Barbs, which were originally
introduced into the country by the Moors ;
and if the Connemara pony were permitted
to revert to the original type, something was
done to re-establish the Spanish—or, perhaps,
it were more accurate to go a step further
back and say the "Barb"—character in the
early thirties

Mr. Samuel Ussher Roberts, C.B., in
course of evidence given before the Royal
Commission on Horse Breeding in Ireland
(1897), stated that he lived for five-and-
twenty years in the west of Galway, and when
in that part of the country, " there was," he
said, " an extremely hardy, wiry class of pony
in the district showing a great deal of the Barb
or Arab blood. Without exception they were
the best animals I ever knew—good shoulders,
good hard legs, good action, and great stamina
   .   .   they were seldom over over 14 hands
2 inches   I never knew one of them to have
a spavin or splint, or to be in any respect
unsound in his wind   .   .   There was a

strong trace of Arab blood, which I always understood arose from the introduction into Connemara of the Barb or Arab by the Martin family many years ago — you could very easily trace it to the Connemara ponies at the time I speak of." In answer to a subsequent question Mr. Ussher Roberts fixed the date of the introduction of the Barb or Arab blood by Colonel Martin at about 1833.

The old stamp of Connemara pony was described by another witness, Mr. R. B Begley, as "long and low with good rein, good back, and well coupled"; but the majority of witnesses from Galway, and those who had personal knowledge of the breed, shared Mr. Ussher Roberts' opinion that it had greatly deteriorated since the middle of the century when the influence of the Barb or Arab sires had died out.

The young animals, it was stated, were collected in droves when about six months old, and hawked about the country for sale, bringing prices ranging from thirty shillings to £3. Many of these were purchased for use in the English coal pits Evidence was forthcoming to show that there are still some good specimens of the breed

Mr John Purdon described a drove he had recently seen in Connemara "They were beautiful mares, I never saw lovelier mares,

about twenty in the drove, and foals with
them. They were the perfect type of a small
thoroughbred mare " These animals were the
property of Mr William Lyons, who kept a
special breed for generations

The falling off in quality was generally
attributed to promiscuous breeding and to
inbreeding. " In some parts of Connemara,"
said Mr. H. A. Robinson, " they just turn a
stallion out loose on the mountains, mongrels
of the very worst description." There is,
however, another factor in the loss of quality,
namely, the terrible straits to which the
peasantry were reduced in the time of the
famine.

A correspondent informs me that in South-
west Cork, in the fifties, nearly all the people
had mare ponies , in West Galway in the sixties
there was scarcely an ass in Connemara west
of Spiddal and Oughterard; and the case in
West Mayo was the same When my informant visited the same districts fifteen or
twenty years later, he observed a remarkable
change " Hard times " had come upon the
people in the interim, and all the small holders
had donkeys instead of ponies ; poverty had
obliged them to sell their mares ; and when
times improved they were too impoverished to
buy new ponies, and replaced those they had
sold with asses.

Under such circumstances, of course, the
better the mare owned by the peasant the
more likely it was to find a purchaser; and
little but the "rag, tag and bobtail" was left
to perpetuate the species. However con-
siderably the remainder depreciated in quality,
they still retained their characteristic hardiness
of constitution and the germs of those qualities
which under better auspices gained the breed
its reputation.

Some of the witnesses who gave evidence
before the Royal Commission mentioned experiments in cross breeding which prove how
well and rapidly the Connemara pony responds
to endeavour to improve it by the introduction
of suitable fresh blood. Mr Samuel Johnston
stated that he had bred one of the best hunters
he ever possessed out of a Connemara mare;
and Mr. R B. Begley described a mare got by
the pure-bred Hackney sire Star of the West
from a "mountainy pony."

This Hackney-Connemara cross could cover
an English mile in three minutes; Mr. Begley
had driven her fifty-six Irish (over seventy-one
statute) miles in a day, and had repeatedly
driven her twelve Irish (over fifteen statute)
miles in an hour and ten minutes, he had won
two prizes with her for action in harness at
the Hollymount Show; and had hunted her
with ten stone on her back. With hounds,

as in the shafts, this really remarkable pony
proved herself able to go and stay, performing
well across country.

These Connemara ponies stand from 12
hands to 14 hands or more. Like other breeds
which run practically wild in mountainous
country, they are above all things hardy, active
and sure-footed in response to the climatic
conditions of their habitat—the climate of
West Galway is the most humid of any spot
in Europe—they grow a thick and shaggy
coat, which is very usually chestnut in colour,
betraying their descent

Although they have lost in size owing to the
conditions of their existence, and are rounder
in the croup, they retain the peculiar ambling
gait which distinguished their Spanish ancestors.
Those with whose breeding care has been
taken, such as the drove belonging to Mr.
William Lyons, of Oughterard, show the
characteristics implanted by the infusion of
Barb blood in their blood-like heads and
clean limbs. Even those which have suffered
through promiscuous breeding conform in their
ugliness and shortcomings to the original type.

For some years past systematic endeavours
to improve the breed have been in progress
The Congested Districts Board, under the
Land Commission of Ireland, introduced small
Hackney stallions whose substance, action and

robust constitution render them particularly
well adapted to correct the effects of weedy
and ill-shaped mares without impairing their
natural hardiness

A few years ago Professor J. Cossar Ewart
was commissioned by the Department of
Agriculture and Technical Instruction for
Ireland to proceed to the Western districts
and make, in consultation with local experts, a
study of the actual condition and possibilities
of the Connemara Pony. Professor Ewart did
so and embodied the results of his inspection
and enquiries in a most interesting paper.*

Professor Ewart was struck with the
strength, endurance and easy paces of the
ponies, as with their intelligence and docility,
and with their capacity for work which would
speedily prove disastrous to horses reared
under less natural conditions. He also
remarked that such striking differences in
size, shape and colour in the ponies that he
was able to describe no fewer than five types,
each one fairly distinct from the other Inasmuch, however, as the Polo Pony Stud Book
Society has adopted as a standard the best
type, we may be content with the following
" Description and definition of the Connemara

: *The Ponies of Connemara*, published at H M
Stationery Office, by Alec Thom, Dublin, in 1900.

Pony," drawn up by the Connemara Pony
Committee, at their meeting held at Clifden,
November 15th, 1901—

"*The Connemara Pony should be intelligent, active, and
enduring, presenting the outline of a long, low, powerful animal,
covering a lot of ground. The action should be good and
straight The Hobbie should be of a yellow-dun, grey or bay
colour, from 13 to 14 hands high, having the croup as high as
the withers; the head should be larger than fine, with large
jaws, the ears small and pointed, the distance from the
occipital crest to the eyes relatively great, and the distance
between the eyes from $7\frac{1}{2}$ to 8 inches The neck should be
strong and of medium length, the shoulders somewhat straight;
the withers of moderate height. the body long and deep (girth
from 63 to 70 inches), mounted on short stout legs (fore-leg
measuring from 31 to 33 inches from elbow to ground); a good
back, powerful loins, slightly drooping, rounded quarters;
well developed breech short below the knee, with flat, hard
bone (measuring from $6\frac{1}{2}$ to $7\frac{1}{2}$ inches under the knee), wide
open, well-formed hoofs.*"

SCOTLAND—PONIES OF THE SOUTH

Scotland from early times has possessed a breed of horses which was held in great esteem , and, as in England, laws were passed from time to time prohibiting their export from the country.

The second parliament of James I. in the year 1406 enacted (cap 31) that no horse of three years old or under should be sent out of Scotland. In 1567 James VI. forbade the export of horses in an Act (Jac. VI , cap 22) whose preface makes specific reference to Bordeaux, from which place there was a great demand for horses

In a curious old book entitled *The Horseman's Honour* or the *Beautie of Horsemanship*, published in the year 1620 by an anonymous writer, we find the following passage :—

" For the horses of Scotland they are much less than those of England, yet not inferiour in goodnesse ; and by reason of their smallnesse they keep few stoned but geld many by which likwise they retaine this saying ' That there is no gelding like those in Scotland,' and they, as the English, are for the most part amblers. Also in Scotland there are a race of small nagges which they call galloways or galloway nagges, which for fine

shape, easie pace, pure mettall and infinit toughnesse
are not short of the best nagges that are bred in any
countrey whatsoever , and for soundnesse in body they
exceede the most races that are extant, as dayly
experience shows in their continuall travels, journeyings
and forehuntings."

Misson,* a French traveller who visited this
country about the year 1695, mentions the
Scottish native stock   He says · " The wild
horses of Scotland are small, but fierce and
vigorous   The way of catching them is to
send a few tame horses among them which are
taught on purpose to draw them into their
company."   From which it is evident that the
ponies were quite as wild as those of the
Welsh hills.

Berenger† says :—

"This kingdom (Scotland) at present encourages a
fleet breed of horses, and the nobility and gentry have
many foreign and other stallions of great value in their
possession with which they cultivate the breed and
improve it with great knowledge and success.   Like the
English they are fond of racing and have a celebrated
course at Leith which is honoured with a royal plate
given by his present Majesty [George III.].

" The wisdom and generosity likewise of the nobility
and gentry have lately erected a riding house in the
City of Edinburgh at their own expense and fixed a
salary upon the person appointed to direct it.

* *Memoirs and Observations*, by M Misson. *Translation.*
London. 1697.

† *The History and Art of Horsemanship*, by Richard
Berenger. Published by Davies and Cadell, London
1771.

"This kingdom has been famous for breeding a peculiar sort of horses called Galloways From the care and attention paid at present to the culture of horses it is to be expected that it will soon be able to send forth numbers of valuable and generous breeds destined to a variety of purposes and equal to all the country being very capable of answering the wishes of the judicious breeder, who need only remember that colts require to be well nourished in winter and sheltered from the severity of a rigorous and changeable sky."

The Galloway, so called from the part of Scotland known by that name, is a diminutive horse resembling the Welsh cob, to which the author of an *Encyclopædia of Agriculture* compares it in a passage quoted on a former page. The breed gradually diminished in number as the advances of law and order deprived the mosstroopers and other predatory border men of a method of livelihood which involved the use of hardy and enduring horses

Before 1800 and during more recent years the Galloways cannot be described either as horses or ponies they played an active part in agricultural work in the lowlands of Scotland.

In localities where no roads existed, and wheeled traffic was impossible, galloways were used not only for riding but for the transport of agricultural produce , as they lacked the weight and strength to draw the two-horse plough, ploughing was done by oxen, but the sledges which held the place of carts and waggons were drawn by the galloways, which

were also used to carry corn and general
merchandise in pots and panniers.

In height the original Galloway was generally under 14 hands. Youatt (second edition,
1846) describes it as from 13 to 14 hands, and
sometimes more , it was a bright bay or brown,
with black legs and small head.

The purposes for which they were used
indicated the desirability of increasing their
height and strength, and with this end in view
cross breeding was commenced somewhere
about the year 1800 and continued for fifty
years. The old Galloway after this period
almost disappeared from all parts of the mainland, and survives only in such remote situa-
tions as the Island of Mull.

98

HIGHLAND PONIES.

The ponies of the more mountainous and
colder northern counties of Scotland are
smaller than those of the south References
to them are few until a hundred or a hundred
and thirty years ago In works on Scottish
agriculture, written about that period, we find
occasional descriptions of these ponies. Soon
after 1775 a Mr. Gilchrist employed on his
farm in Sutherlandshire as many as ten
"garrons" to carry. peats from the hills and
seaweed from the shore. These burdens were
carried in crates or panniers :—

"The little creatures do wonders, they set out at
peep of day and never halt till the work of the day be
finished—going 48 miles "*

In 1812 Captain Henderson† wrote —

"Upon the extensive farms of the east coast of
Sutherlandshire there are large horses kept for the
plough and cart, but in the other parts of the district
the native breeds of ' garrons' are used for the plough
four abreast, and in some cases three abreast. Four

* *Husbandry in Scotland.* Published by Creech, Edinburgh, 1784.
† *A General View of the Agriculture of Sutherlandshire,*
by Captain J. Henderson. 1812.

of these garrons are generally kept to plough from 8
to 10 acres of arable land   Their food is the pasture of
the fields and moors summer and winter, except that in
severe weather they are kept in stables or sheds where
they are fed with straw, and during the spring labour
they get some meadow hay.   Their price is from 4 to
10 guineas, according to size and quality, they are
from 11 hands to 13 hands high; their colours black,
brown or grey."

At one time, Captain Henderson says, a
great many brood mares were kept by the
farmers, who sold the young stock when about
14 months old to travelling dealers.   The
dealers used to take these young ones to
the Orkneys, and usually exchanged them
for five- and six-year-old ponies bred in the
islands which they sold at a profit in the
Caithness markets in the late summer.   This
interchange of blood could not but be beneficial to the breed.   The great spread of sheep
farms early in the last century almost entirely
stopped the pony breeding industry.

At the present time the most conspicuous
field of utility open to the Scottish pony is
that offered by the grouse-moors and deer-
forests, though in the close season general
farm and draught work affords them employ-
ment.   A pony of from 13 hands to 14 hands
may be strong enough for a man of average
weight to ride on the grouse-moor, but for
deer-stalking a sturdy cob of from 14 hands

to 14 hands 3 inches is necessary, a smaller
animal is not equal to the task of carrying a
heavy man or a 17-stone stag over the rough
hills and valleys among which his work lies.

Mr J. H. Munro Mackenzie contributes a
brief but informing essay on the Highland
Ponies to vol vii of *Polo Pony Society's
Stud Book.* He states that the breeding of
these ponies has for years been so greatly
neglected that it is a difficult matter to write
a history of the breed, but his remarks furnish
a valuable addition to the few details it has
been possible to collect from other sources.
Mr. Munro Mackenzie says :—

"After long study and observation I have come to the
conclusion that the original Highland Pony was a small
animal from 12 hands 2 inches to 13 hands 2 inches,
such as is now to be seen on the Island of Barra and
some of the small islands off the west coast of Scotland.
One strong reason I have for this conclusion is the great
number of ponies that were bred in the Highlands in
old times. In a record I have of my own property (by
no means a large one) I find that in the year 1770 nearly
80 ponies were kept, and taking into consideration the
very large stock of cattle kept at the same time, the
ponies must have been very small and hardy, as the
cattle would be sure to have the best part of the
ground

"Highland Ponies may be divided into three classes —

"First, the small ponies of Barra and the outer
islands running from 12 hands 2 inches to 13 hands
2 inches; they have good hard legs and feet, head
rather large and plain, and shoulders a bit straight, but
are hardy, useful little animals, well suited to stand
exposure and poor feeding, and when brought on to good

keep it is quite wonderful how they grow and improve
Colours black, bay, and brown, with a few duns and
greys. I have occasionally seen some very beautiful
little ponies from the outer islands, but these are
generally to be traced to an Arab cross.

"Second, what might be called the high-class riding
pony of the West Highlands and Islands, running from
13 hands 2 inches to 14 hands 2 inches This class of
pony has almost died out; they were to be found in
Mull, Tiree, Skye and Uist, and some parts of the
western mainland These ponies show a very strong
cross of Arab blood, which is accounted for in several
ways, it is said they are descended from Eastern horses
wrecked from the Spanish Armada, and also that a
number of Highland officers brought their Arab chargers
home with them and bred from them. These ponies
have beautiful heads and good shoulders, in fact, are
good all over, and of riding type famous for staying
through long journeys under heavy weights and on poor
keep, the only pity is that so few of them are left.
Colours black, brown, dun and grey, with a few bays,
the duns and greys generally show most Arab blood
I have known many duns and greys with quite an Arab
look in which I cannot trace any direct Arab cross for
generations."

The Arab character referred to might well
be expected to continue long after all definite
record of an Arab cross has been lost. We
have it in the Connemara ponies and in other
breeds; and the high antiquity of the Arab
ensures the lasting effects of its influence upon
any breed with which it may be crossed.
Mr. Munro Mackenzie continues —

"The third class is what are often called Garrons,
they run a good deal bigger than the former classes
Some are found up to 15 hands; they are more the

horses of Perthshire and the Central Highlands than
of the West Highlands and Islands. I am of opinion
that they were originally bred from small ponies crossed
with larger horses brought into the Highlands with
troops during the unsettled times They have good
game heads, bold eyes, shoulder a bit straight, and
back long, with the best of legs and feet, a good tuft
of hair on the heel, and often a very well set on tail.
Colours brown, black, dun, grey, and a few bays.
This is a most useful breed to keep up, as they are fit
for all the work on Highland farms, are first-rate deer
and game carriers, and with a little improvement in
shoulders they would be capital riding ponies for hill
work. Lastly, being roomy, heavy animals, with hardy
constitutions, they are most valuable as foundation
stock to cross with blood to produce weight-carrying
ponies of high class."

The description of the Highland Pony,
drawn up at a meeting of the District Committee, held in the showyard of the Highland
and Agricultural Society at Inverness, on
July 7th, 1901, and adopted by the Polo Pony
Stud Book Society, is as follows —

"*It shall be of great substance and power, with firm, hard
feet, flat bone, and short covered ribs. The eyes should be bold
and prominent, but with a kindly expression. Height up to
14 hands 2 inches.*"

CHILD'S SHETLAND PONY.

The property of Sir WALTER GILBEY. Bart.

SCOTLAND—SHETLAND PONIES.

The Shetland pony stands upon a footing different from all those breeds noticed in the foregoing pages. In it we have a pony whose characteristics are equally valuable to it as a wild animal and as one in a state of domestication It is the only one of our half-wild breeds which gains nothing from an infusion of alien blood; its value depends upon the careful preservation of distinctive peculiarities of size and make, which fit it above all others for special purposes.

The origin of the "Sheltie," like that of the other breeds of Great Britain and Ireland, is unknown. Mr. James Goudie, whose essay on *The Early History of the Shetland Pony* is published in the first volume of the *Shetland Pony Stud Book*, thinks there is every likelihood that it was brought to the islands from Scotland at some very early period.

The "Bressay Stone," a sculptured slab which was discovered in Bressay in 1864, bears, among other designs in low relief, the figure of a horse on which a human figure is seated.

"As this monument is admitted by authorities on the
subject to belong to a period before the Celtic Christi-
anity of the islands disappeared under the shock of
Norwegian invasion [A.D. 872], it may be inferred . .
that the animal was known and probably found in the
islands at this period."

Early writers state that the Scandinavian
invaders introduced the foundation stock some
time prior to the fifteenth century. Buchanan
makes passing reference to the Orkney and
Shetland ponies in his *History of Scotland*,
written three centuries ago, but the first
description which has completeness to recommend it is that of Brand, who visited the
islands in 1700 and wrote *A Brief Description
of Orkney, Zetland, Pightland, Firth and
Caithness*, which was published at Edinburgh
in the following year This author writes —

"They are of a less size than the Orkney Horses, for
some will be but 9, others 10 nives or hand-breadths
high, and they will be thought big Horses there if 11,
and although so small yet they are full of vigour and
life, and some not so high as others often prove to be
the strongest . Summer or winter they never
come into an house but run upon the mountains, in
some places in flocks, and if any time in Winter the
storm be so great that they are straitened for food they
will come down from the Hills when the ebb is in the
sea and eat the seaware . . which Winter storms
and scarcity of fodder puts them out of ease and bringeth
them so very low that they recover not their strength
till St. John's Mass-day, the 24th June, when they are at
their best They will live to a considerable age, as
twenty-six, twenty-eight, or thirty years, and they will
be good riding horses in twenty-four, especially they'le

be the more vigorous and live the longer if they be four years old before they be put to work. Those of a black colour are judged to be the most durable and the pyeds often prove not so good ; they have been more numerous than they now are."

Bengie, in his *Tour in Shetland* (1870), after remarking on their sure-footedness and hardiness of constitutions, suggests that the sagacity, spirit and activity for which they are remarkable may be due to the freedom of the life they live on the hills "They are sprightly and active as terriers, sure-footed as mules and patient as donkeys." They stand, he adds, at the head of the horse tribe as the most intelligent and faithful of them all ; and he compares the intelligence of the Sheltie with that of the Iceland pony, much to the advantage of the former.

Mr Robert Brydon, of Seaham Harbour, says they are "shorter in the leg than any other kind, and at the same time they are wider in the body and shorter in the back, with larger bones, thighs and arms ; and therefore are comparatively stronger and able to do with ease as much work as average ponies of other breeds a hand higher."

The Shetland Stud Book Society will register no pony whose height exceeds 10 hands 2 inches, and the average height may be taken as 10 hands : many do not exceed 9 hands, and a lady who wrote an account of a

visit to Shetland in 1840 speaks of one reared
by Mr. William Hay, of Hayfield, which was
only 26 inches, or 6 hands 2 inches high! It
is, however, unusual to find a pony measuring
less than 8 hands at the shoulder, and we may
perhaps doubt whether the 26-inch specimen
was full-grown.

In colour the Shetlander varies : bays,
browns and dullish blacks are most common ;
sometimes these hues are relieved by white
markings, and occasionally white specimens
occur , piebalds are rare   The coat in winter
is long, close and shaggy, fit protection against
the inclemency of the weather the pony endures
without cover or shelter : in spring the heavy
winter coat is shed, and in the summer months
the hair is short and sleek

In former times it was customary to hobble
the ponies ; but this practice, which must have
done much to spoil their naturally good action,
has been abandoned for many years

It is now usual to give the ponies a ration of
hay in the winter months when the vegetation
is covered deep with snow, and thus the losses
by starvation, which formerly were heavy in
severe winters, are obviated   Otherwise the
Sheltie's conditions of life to-day differ little
from those that prevailed three centuries ago.
Mr. Meiklejohn, of Bressay, states that in
April, generally, the crofters turn their ponies

out upon the common pasture lands, and leave them to their own devices On common pastures where there are no stallions the mares are caught for service and tethered until the foal is born and can follow freely, when mother and foal are turned out again

In autumn when crops have been carried the ponies come down from the hills to their own townships, where they feed on the patches of fresh grass which have been preserved round the cultivated areas The nights being now cold, they remain in the low-lying lands, sheltering under the lee of the yard walls , and " when winter has more fully set in the pony draws nearer his owner's door, and in most cases is rewarded with his morning sheaf on which, with seaweed and what he continues to pick off the green sward, the hardy animal manages to eke out a living until the time rolls round again that he is turned on the hill pasture, never being under a roof in his life."

At one period the ponies were apparently regarded almost as public property , for, among the " Acts and Statutes of the Lawting Sheriff and Justice Courts of Orkney and Shetland," was one passed in the year 1612 and frequently renewed, which forbade the " ryding and uther manis hors without licence and leave of the awner," under penalty of fine ; and also provided that "quhasoever sall be tryet

or fund to stow or cut ane uther man's hors
taill sall be pwinischit as a theif at all rigour
in exempill of utheris to commit the lyke."

The number of ponies on the islands has
increased somewhat during the last ten years,
owing no doubt to the islanders having realised
that the industry of pony breeding deserves
attention. Ten years ago the returns showed
a decline owing to the steadily growing
demand from without. The latest available
Government returns are those of 1901.

In 1901 the statistics given were :—

Horses used solely for agriculture (including mares kept for breeding) . .	3,071
Unbroken horses 1 year and over	1,799
,, ,, under 1 year .. .	1,094
	5,964

It is to be observed that by far the greater
number of the " horses " are Shetland ponies.

The ponies are little used for farm work in
the Shetlands ; they carry loads of peat from
the hills to the crofts, and apart from this are
used only for riding ; they are beyond question
the most wonderful weight-carriers in the
world, a 9-hand pony being able to carry with
the greatest ease a full-grown man over bad
ground and for long distances

They owe their value to the combination of
minuteness and strength, which renders them
peculiarly suitable for draught work in coal

mines. Many ponies will travel thirty miles a
day, to and fro in the seams, drawing a load,
tilt and coals included, of from 12 to 14 cwt.
The Sheltie's lot underground is admittedly a
hard one, but " as use becomes second nature,"
he becomes contented, and his tractable dis-
position ensures for him kindly treatment at
the hands of the boy who has him in charge.

These ponies, says Mr. Brydon, were first
used in the coal pits of the North of England
about the year 1850. Horse ponies from
three to five years old could then be purchased
for £4 10s each delivered at the collieries.
Since that time prices have risen enormously,
though for the smallest animals they fluctuate
from time to time in sympathy with the price
of coal.

As the cause of the influence of the coal
market upon the price of Shetland ponies is
perhaps not quite obvious, it must be explained
that the chief value of these little animals
is their ability to work in the low galleries
of thin-seamed pits, when the price of coal
sinks to a certain point these thin seams
cannot be profitably worked, the pits are " laid
in," or temporarily closed, and the ponies
withdrawn.

In 1891 the average yearling was worth
£15 and a two-year-old £18, while full-grown
ponies were scarcely procurable. In 1898 a

four-year-old could be bought at from £15
to £21, owing to the depression in the price
of coals and the suspension of work in thin-
seamed pits.

It will be understood that only small animals
of the commoner sort suitable for pit work are
affected by the coal market Ponies of the
right stamp with good pedigree and suitable
for the stud have in many cases changed hands
at £40 to £50; and in some cases even
more.

Mare ponies of good pedigree also command
high prices, at the Londonderry sale, mares
have been sold at an average of £19 per
head; but the average obtained for lower
grade mares did not exceed six guineas per
head

The docility and good temper of the
Shetland pony make him, above all, the best
and most trustworthy mount for a child. It
is the exception to find a vicious Sheltie   Mr.
Brydon says he has never known a Sheltie
withdrawn from a pit as wicked or unmanage-
able, withdrawal for such reasons being very
frequent with ponies of other breeds.

It may be observed that about 1850 there
were a number of Shelties in Windsor Park,
which were used to do various kinds of work.

During recent years a demand for mares
for breeding purposes has grown up in America,

much to the advantage of the crofter, who finds a market in the colliery districts for horse ponies only.

Many attempts have been made to increase the size of the Sheltie About the middle of the last century Norwegian pony stallions were introduced into Dunrossness, with the result that a distinct variety was established and still continues ; this is called the Sumburgh breed ; in size these ponies range from 12 hands to 13 hands 2 inches.

Another variety known as the Fetlar breed owes its origin to the introduction by Sir Arthur Nicolson of a Mustang stallion named Bolivar previous to 1850; the Fetlar ponies run from 11 to 13 hands, and are described as remarkably handsome, swift and spirited, but less tractable than the pure Shetlander.

The Sumburgh and Fetlar varieties deserve mention only as experiments ; the result having been to increase the height of the pony, it follows, after what has been said on a former page, that these cross-bred animals are of comparatively small value.

Far more importance attaches to the efforts which have been made to improve the pure breed while preserving its diminutive size. The Marquis of Londonderry, nearly twenty-five years ago, acquired grazings on Bressay and Moss Islands ; and having procured the best stock obtainable from all over the Shetlands, began breeding on judicious and methodical lines

Twelve or fifteen mares with a carefully selected stallion were placed in an enclosure, and the young stock, after weaning, were turned out on the hills, they were hand-fed in winter, but never given the protection of a roof, whereby their natural hardiness was preserved.*

The Marquis of Zetland in Unst, and Mr. Bruce in Fair Isle, follow a somewhat similar method of mating and rearing On Northmavine Messrs. Anderson and Sons have done much to promote the interests of the breed by purchasing good stallions, often at Lord Londonderry's annual Seaham Harbour Sale, and distributing these over the common pastures. The benefits which have accrued from this policy are very marked ; and though the crofters yield to the temptation of high prices, and sell their best animals for export, the endeavours of the gentlemen named above to maintain the quality of the breed in its

---

* While the first edition of this book was passing through the press Lord Londonderry gave up his breeding stud on Bressay, the ponies having been brought to Seaham Harbour and there sold The farm and lands occupied by the Marquis's stud have passed into the hands of Mr. Manson, a well-known farmer and breeder of Shetland ponies

native habitat cannot fail to largely counteract the evil results of such sales.

Among the studs on the mainland one of the best known, perhaps, is that of the Countess of Hopetoun at Linlithgow Her ladyship's success has been due in no small measure to that beautiful little sire the Monster This pony is a perfect example of the Shetland stallion , he was first in the class for Shetland ponies under 10 hands 2 inches at the Royal Agricultural Society's Show in 1895, at Darlington. Lord Londonderry's Excellent has also been a successful prize-taker. The pony Good Friday, from the Elsenham stud, has won numerous prizes, among them five firsts at the London shows.

Another famous breeder is Mrs. Hope Johnstone, of Edenbridge, Kent, whose successes in the showyard lend weight to her views on the subject. Mrs. Hope Johnstone has been kind enough to send the following notes on rearing Shetlands in the South of England ·—

"It is an error to suppose that increased height is obtained by breeding Shetland ponies in England. I have a theory that such increased height is induced by the endeavours that are made to keep down the size by starving the dams and foals. A Shetland which is kept short of food from foalhood to its third or fourth year grows tall, narrow, long in the leg and also weak-legged If the foal is done well from the time of birth until it reaches full growth it thickens out all ways—spreads

in every direction *except* in height ; and attains to the
roundness and symmetry of shape so characteristic of
the breed.

"The character of Lord Londonderry's splendid stud
on the Island of Bressay, Shetland, carried out this
theory   His animals, while less tall than the ponies of
the neighbouring crofters, showed greater width, bulk
and superior bone, owing to their more liberal diet *
I have now a horse pony bred by Lord Londonderry.
he stands 8 hands ½ inch, and is six years old , this pony
combines the make, shape and thickness of a Clydesdale
with the action of a Hackney.

"The English climate is thought too mild for these
ponies   This is a mistake · the climate of the Shetland
Islands in some important respects is far less severe ,
it is very much more equitable, there being less difference between the extremes of temperature in winter
and summer , certainly the Shetland climate is more
moist than ours, but the islands are not subject to our
rasping east winds, and the boisterous gales of the
north are less penetrating than an east wind. Owing
to this mistaken idea about climates, some English
breeders think that Shetland ponies which remain out
in winter do not require the shelter of a shed

"Their belief is that in the Shetlands the ponies are
given no shelter and are left out in all weathers. It is
true that they enjoy no *artificial* shelter , but it is important to know that on every part of Shetland the ponies
can find dry sandy beds which afford comfortable lying.
There are no such resting places in English pastures
and it is the lying out on thick, wet grass, in the cold
and damp that distresses them , the shelter of a shed
is therefore most necessary

"The ponies thrive splendidly on moors by the coast.
Such lands may *look* bare of herbage, bleak and wind-
swept, but there is that variety of food, different mosses,
beds of reeds, young heather, grass, &c , &c., which
helps to make them what they should be ; and on these
moors, too, the dry bed is always obtainable.

* See p 112

"I do not consider that the Shetlands in England breed with the same certainty as they do in the islands or on a sea-moor in Scotland. The extra artificial food, lack of variety of herbage, and want of roaming space in English pastures militate against their breeding truly to type. If one may so speak the Shetland ponies have a kind of objection to 'breeding in captivity,' in which they resemble no other breed of domestic animal.

"The action of English-bred Shetlands may leave something to be desired, this is no doubt due to the fact that they are reared, as a rule, on fairly level ground, and miss, as foals, the rough, boulder-strewn ground and long heather which teaches them to pick up their feet and bend their hocks No English stud of Shetlands can long maintain the characteristic action of the breed unless corrected by the importation of island or Scottish sea-moor stock—especially by fresh stallions.

"In my personal experience I find that a pony loses action from *constant showing*. I can offer no reason for this unless it is that the noise and excitement of show-yard life wears them out and they are bored by it. If judges could be persuaded to admire ponies in ordinary condition and not fed up into mountains of flesh they would last longer and probably keep their action better. The great objection to showing is that the animals must be made so fat, otherwise it is hopeless to expect a prize."

Among Mrs. Hope Johnstone's successful ponies may be mentioned the 9 hands black mare, Sapphire, who won eleven first prizes in the years 1897-1901, at the best shows in the kingdom, including the Royal and the Highland and Agricultural Shows Emerald, mouse-coloured, 9 hands 1 inch, has won thirteen first prizes during the years 1899-1902, including firsts in saddle and harness

classes at the Madison Square, New York,
Show in 1901 Topaz, a black mare bred
by Lord Londonderry, won in 1902 six firsts,
including one at the Royal, and the championship at the Highland and Agricultural, and
a championship as the best Shetland at the
Perth Show Among the many prizes won
by her Skylark was the championship at the
Highland Show of 1901. Mrs. Hope Johnstone, it will have been observed, has achieved
the feat of taking the championship for the
best Shetland pony at the Highland and Agricultural Society's Show for three successive
years—each time with a mare

Mrs Hope Johnstone draws attention to a
fact which has not before been brought under
the writer's notice, namely, the frequency with
which the mare of the Shetland breed possesses
tushes as well developed as those of the horse.
Some of the mares endowed thus with tushes,
she further informs me, will not breed at all,
some are uncertain breeders, and others, again,
breed as readily as mares with ordinary
mouths

Mr. James Bruce has a drove of Shetland
ponies at Inverquhomery, Longside, Aberdeen-
shire These are descended from two mares
and a stallion imported in the year 1889
Five years ago Mr Bruce replenished his
breeding stock by the purchase of five more

mares   A noteworthy feature of this stud is the colour, which in every case is chestnut, Mr. Bruce's 1889 importations being of that rare colour among Shelties.

Since the establishment of the *Shetland Pony Stud Book*, several studs have been founded in Scotland and England

ARAB PONIES.

The Arab has played so large and important a part in building up our English breeds of light horses that a few remarks on the Arab in England seem to be desirable In the first place the reader may be again reminded that the numerous Arabs, Barbs and Turkish horses —the two latter being local branches of pure Arab stock—were not *horses* as we understand the word, but *ponies*, their height ranging from 14 hands to 14 hands 2 inches at the most.

It would not be difficult to trace the importation of Eastern sires into England from a remote date. It is, however, only necessary to record their introduction some three centuries back, when in the reign of King James I. (1603-1625) the importations of Eastern sires became sufficiently numerous to make their mark upon our native stock

There is abundant evidence to show that we had good racehorses in England before the "Arab invasion", but, as Mr Osborne* says, it was not until after the arrival of the cele-

* *Horse Breeders' Handbook*, by John Osborne. Published by Edmund Seale, London. 4th Edition.

brated Eastern sires in the early years of the period 1700-1800 that the Arabian spirit and symmetry became prominently developed in the English horse.

King James on many occasions received presents of horses from foreign sovereigns and nobles on one occasion he was given no fewer than twenty-seven Neapolitan " coursers," of which eleven were stallions; this breed had a very strong strain of Arab or Barb blood

In view of King James's love of horses and racing Mr. Osborne is justified in his supposition that Sir Thomas Edmonds, an experienced traveller and ambassador, doubtless acquired for the King many Eastern horses other than the half-dozen Barbs which he brought to England in 1617 and which were sent direct to the Royal stud at Newmarket.

English horses at this period were making rapid improvement, as we learn from the demand for them which came from the Continent, but we cannot trace this improvement to any particular sire or sires. The Markham Arabian is the one animal of which we have any particulars, and that horse did nothing on the racecourse or at the stud, so far as the records show, to entitle him to rank among the good Eastern horses imported.

It may be well here to correct the error concerning the price paid for this horse which has been generally adopted by writers on the subject The statement occurs in the 4th edition of vol. i of the *General Stud Book* that " King James I bought an Arabian of Mr Markham, a merchant, for 500 gs " This assertion, which Sir Ernest Clarke attributes, and without doubt accurately, to a passage in the Duke of Newcastle's famous work, is incorrect Sir Ernest Clarke caused search to be made and found the following in the Exchequer of Receipt Order Books preserved in the Public Record Office :—

" 11 July 1616 An account of such horses bought for the Kings and Queen's Majestys service since the 11 July 1616 and how the sum of 400*l*. impressed to the Rt Hon the Earl of Buckingham, Master of your Majesty's Horse, towards the buying of horse for your Majesty's use hath been disbursed viz —

" Item, the 20th of December 1616, paid to Master Markham for the Arabian Horse for His Majesty's own use 154 0 0*l*

" Item, the same day paid to a man that brought the same Arabian Horse and kept him 11 0 0*l* "

The same accounts give the prices of numerous geldings bought for the Royal stables ; these range from £12 to £70 : the latter sum being paid for " a chestnut hunting gelding for H M own use." The sum of £154 for the Markham Arabian was therefore an exceptionally high price and, as Sir Ernest Clarke observes, £500 for a horse in those days is quite inconceivable

The first Eastern sire which is known to have made his mark at the stud was the Helmsley Turk imported by the Duke of Buckingham in Charles I's reign (1625-1645). "His blood has been chiefly transmitted to our time through Old Merlin, Blunderbuss, the Bolton Starling, the Bolton Sweepstakes, and the Blacklegs mare", the last named being the dam of Marske, the sire of Eclipse.

The troubles which brought about the murder of Charles I in the year 1645, and the disturbed times which followed, did a great deal to injure the English horse-breeding industry, the Royal Studs and those formed by loyal noblemen were dispersed and the horses purchased by foreigners. It is very probable also that the records of breeding were destroyed When peace was at length restored attention was once more devoted to horse breeding.

Cromwell established a stud of his own, and his stud-master, a Mr Place, who is said to have been an excellent judge of horseflesh and a successful breeder, brought to England a horse named Place's White Turk, which wrought lasting influence This animal owes his fame as a sire chiefly to his daughters, to one or other of which such famous horses as Snap and Matchem trace their descent.

The improvement produced by imported

horses so far had been more or less incidental;
in other words the Arabs, Barbs or Turks had
been purchased for the primary purpose of
racing, their use at the stud afterwards being
in the nature of an afterthought

It was reserved for King Charles II (1660-
1685) to purchase stock from abroad for the
definite purpose of breeding. Soon after he
had taken his seat on the throne he sent Sir
John Fenwick, master of the horse and a
prominent supporter of the turf, to purchase
in foreign countries both stallions and mares
for breeding purposes. There is unfortunately
no record existing of Sir John Fenwick's
mission, and we do not know whether he
bought Arabs, Barbs, or Turkish horses; but
this is of no great importance, inasmuch as the
three breeds known to our ancestors by these
names were so nearly allied   The blood of at
least one stallion thus imported whose origin
appears in his name, "The Fenwick Barb,"
occurs in many horses of the present day
through The Bald Galloway, whose dam was
a daughter of the Fenwick Barb.

It is to the mares imported by Charles II.,
the "Royal Mares" as they have ever since
been called, that the English horses owed so
much. The mare called Dodsworth's Dam,
which dropped a foal a short time after her
landing in this country, is entitled to the

credit that attaches to the dam of a great
horse. Dodsworth's progeny, both sons and
daughters, distinguished themselves at the
stud. Brown Farewell, a great great grand-
daughter of Dodsworth, produced the dam of
Young Cade and Matchem.

On the death of Charles II. the mares
appear to have been sold to various purchasers
and found their way to various parts of the
country ; they can be traced by the practice of
their new owners, who distinguished them by
such names as the Sedbury Royal Mare and
D'Arcy's Royal Mare "D'Arcy's Royal
Mares" are so numerous that it would seem
as though Lord D'Arcy and his family were
the purchasers of the greater number, to which
circumstance Mr. Joseph Osborne attributes
the excellence of the Sedbury Stud, "which
gave so many good horses to the British
Turf."

Lord D'Arcy used in his stud two sires, the
White D'Arcy Turk and the D'Arcy Yellow
Turk, which he imported himself. The blood
of the former, through his son, Wilkes Old
Hautboy, runs in the veins of some of our best
modern strains through the dam of Snake.
The D'Arcy Yellow Turk mated with the
D'Arcy Royal Mares was also a highly suc-
cessful sire. Both, in Mr Joseph Osborne's
words, " were sires of great value, and their

names are to be found at the root of all our best pedigrees."

Curwen's Bay Barb, more frequently called The Bay Barb, in recognition of his outstanding excellence, and the Thoulouse Barb, were also brought to England in Charles II's reign, and it is worth noticing that a daughter of Old Spot threw to the Bay Barb a foal named Mixbury, which stood only 13 hands 2 inches and became the best small horse of his day.

During the reign of James II. the only notable Eastern importation was the Stradling or Lester Turk, who became the sire of Coneyskins and Snake, to name his most celebrated sons.

Many good Eastern horses were imported during the reign of William and Mary. The name of the Byerly Turk, brought home by Captain Byerly and used by him as a charger throughout the Irish wars, is familiar to all as one of the great foundation sires of the breed of racehorses.

Chillaby, a Barb bought in Morocco by Mr. Marshall for King William, was another, but is "better known for his ferocity and subsequent friendship with a lamb than for his achievements as a sire."

Greyhound, one of the best and most prepotent sires of his time, was foaled soon after the arrival in England of his dam, Slugey or Sloughby, one of Mr. Marshall's purchases for the Royal Stud. Greyhound was sent to Yorkshire after a period of service at Hampton Court, and he got many good performers on the turf, it is instructive to note, however, that his merits were transmitted through the female line : "it was through three of Greyhound's unnamed daughters that the British Turf and stud chiefly benefited," as Mr. Osborne informs us These three mares were the property of Mr. Crofts, of Barforth, Yorkshire, a famous breeder.

The Selaby Turk was another valuable importation of this period : and again we find that, like Greyhound and many other of the Eastern sires, the name of the Selaby Turk has been chiefly perpetuated through his daughters The Akaster Turk, sire of many distinguished mares, and the Honeywood Arabian who got the two True Blues, also deserve mention.

It was during Queen Anne's reign that the great influx of Eastern sires took place .

"About the time of the arrival of the Darley Arabian in Yorkshire there arose an extraordinary rivalry among the wealthy noblemen and gentlemen resident in the three great Ridings and in the neighbouring counties for the possession of Eastern blood, which not only increased as time went on but extended to other parts of this Kingdom ; and to this circumstance is chiefly due the immense improvement that took place in our breed of horses during the early part of the last century" (Osborne)

Besides the Darley Arabian, from whom our best hackneys are descended through Flying Childers, there arrived in England the Leedes Arabian, the Oglethorpe Arabian, the Southern White-legged Barb, and some twenty more Eastern sires. Mr. Osborne's valuable work contains a list of the Eastern horses which are known to have been imported from James I's time ; this list includes the names of 90 Arab sires, 36 Barbs, 32 Turks, 4 Persians, and 2 horses of unknown foreign origin, 164 sires altogether.

It was by crossing these horses—or ponies as we should consider them nowadays, inasmuch as few could have exceeded 14 hands 1 inch—with our native stock that our ancestors obtained animals which could run three heats of four miles each on the same day, carrying weights we should regard as absurd, if not cruel For example, Queen Anne's Gold Cup of 100 guineas, run on Wednesday, July 28th, 1714, was for six-year-old horses carrying 12 stone each

The importation into England of Arabs and Barbs fell off greatly during the latter half of the eighteenth and during the nineteenth century Some were imported for breeding purposes, as we have seen in previous chapters, and others were sent to the reigning sovereign as gifts, but for many years, until the intro-

duction of the game of polo created a demand
for small, strong and active animals, the Arabs
brought to this country were few. When polo
became established in England officers returning from service in India and Egypt had
inducement to bring home their best Arab and
Syrian Arab ponies with them, and when
these were withdrawn from the polo-ground
some of the best, such as Lord Harrington's
well-known Barb, Awfully Jolly, were put to
the stud. Since the close of the South African
war a number of good Arab ponies have been
brought home by officers returning from the
Cape.

Mr Everard R. Calthrop, Wanstead, Essex,
is the owner of Rohan, whose portrait is
here given. Rohan, black, 14 hands 1¾
inches, is registered in the last edition of the
Polo Pony Stud Book He has regularly
carried 16 stone

Messrs. Schwimmer, of Buda Pesth, give
his pedigree :—

"His sire, 'Bohar the Famous,' is celebrated throughout Arabia, and it is stated that in 1898 Rohan was
forwarded to H.I.M the Sultan of Turkey from the
Province of Baghdad as the best horse of his year. At
the command of His Majesty and in recognition of the
high quality of Hungarian horses supplied by them to
the Turkish Government during the late Turko-Greek
war, he was presented to Messrs Schwimmer, of Buda
Pesth, by His Excellency Haki Pasha (Aide de Camp to
H I M the Sultan, and Commandant of the 1st Regi-

ment of Cavalry), a special Irade being signed by His
Majesty to authorise his exportation from Constan-
tinople In November, 1900, he was presented by
Messrs Schwimmer to Mr. E R Calthrop, M.Inst
C E , his present owner. He is believed to be the
highest caste Arab stallion imported in England for the
last hundred years."

Rohan, in a word, is an admirable representative of breed to which we owe so much
It is customary to disparage the speed of the
Arab: admittedly the English thoroughbred
is very much the faster, particularly over a
short distance , but it is absurd to compare
the speed of a 14 hands 1 inch horse, which
for centuries has been bred for real work, with
that of a 15 hands 1 inch to 16 hands horse
which has been most carefully bred for speed
and nothing else.

It is not for speed that the Arab is valued ;
it is for his extraordinary staying power,
soundness of constitution, and the power,
derived from the high antiquity of his race,
to bestow these qualities upon the descendants.
A few instances of the Arab's ability to
perform long journeys and his extraordinary
recuperative power which enables him to travel
long distances day after day have been given
in another book,* to which the reader may be
referred

---

* *Small Horses in Warfare*, by Sir Walter Gilbey,
Bart 2s. Messrs. Vinton and Co , Ltd 1900.

ARAB PONY ROHAN.

It has been remarked that though all the nations of Europe have enjoyed opportunities at least equal to our own of procuring Eastern sires for stud purposes, the introduction of Eastern blood into England has produced results incomparably better than it has done anywhere else, as witness the eagerness with which our best sires have always been, and still are, purchased by foreign stud masters

This superiority of the English thoroughbred cannot be due to chance; it indicates that our soil and climate are above all others in Europe suitable for horse breeding.

Perhaps the English thoroughbreds may also owe their superior speed to the fabulous expenditure in selecting, breeding and managing them for upwards of 200 years

The points it is desirable to make, however, are these: that we have at the present day, more particularly in some of our native ponies, the strain of blood which mingled so happily with the Arabian, Barb and Turk from the time of James I. to that of Queen Anne; and that our soil and climate are unchanged

Therefore, since the crossing of Eastern and native blood two or three hundred years ago produced a stout little horse, able to gallop far and fast under heavy weights, the same cross, if judiciously made, will produce a horse or pony equally good now.

9

USES AND CHARACTERISTICS OF
THE PONY.

It would be difficult to name a class of work in which the pony is not employed. He is used by all, from the sovereign to the peasant and costermonger. It is rare that a meet of hounds is not attended by a sprinkling of ponies carrying boys and young ladies, and it is safe to assert that every master of hounds and every finished rider who takes his own line across country served his apprenticeship to the saddle on the back of a pony. Those men who do not learn to ride in early boyhood, when a pony is the only possible mount, seldom completely master the art in later life ; hence we meet few good horsemen who have not received their first riding lessons on a steady pony.

There is no stamp of vehicle which is not drawn by ponies Her late Majesty, for many years, drove a pony in her garden-chair, in double or single harness we find the pony driven in victoria, dog-cart, governess cart, and Irish car, in the tradesman's light van and in the market cart, drawing wares of every

Drawn by J. Doyle.   Engraved on wood by F. Babbage.

H.R.H. THE PRINCESS VICTORIA IN HER PONY PHAETON.

description; in the itinerant fishmonger's, coster's and hawker's nondescript vehicle.

The country clergyman and doctor would be in sore straits without the 13 hands pony, which does a horse's work on one-half a horse's feed, and requires no more stable attendance than the gardener or handy man can spare time to give him

Pony racing has been recently re-established as a sport after temporary suspension, due to no shortcoming on the pony's side.

As shown in the foregoing pages, the labours of the pony are not confined to saddle and harness, in some parts of the country he is still used for pack-work, carrying agricultural produce and peats from the hills and moorlands to the farmstead; and in the low seams of the coal-pits which the horse cannot enter he is indispensable.

Large though our native stock of ponies is, we do not breed them in numbers nearly sufficient for our needs, and each year brings thousands of small cheap ponies to our ports from Norway, Sweden and Russia. These, like the gangs purchased from breeders on Exmoor and elsewhere, are driven from one fair to another, to be sold by twos and threes all over the country to persons who cannot afford to keep a horse, but are obliged to provide themselves with a cheap and useful beast for draught or carriage.

The pony foaled and brought up on the hills and wastes develops ability, like other wild animals, to look after himself, and the intelligence so evolved is transmitted to generations born in domestication. The same causes operate to furnish the pony's stronger constitution and greater soundness ; greater soundness not only in limb but also organic ; roaring and whistling are unknown in the pony, common as they are in the horse

The horse, foaled and reared in captivity, with every precaution taken for his security, is not called upon to take care of himself, and therefore his mental faculties remain to a great extent undeveloped.

This superiority of constitution accounts for the marked superiority of the pony over the horse in endurance The small and compact horse is always a better stayer than the large, loosely-built animal, and in the pony we find the merits of compactness at their highest

Numberless instances of pony endurance might be quoted, but two or three will suffice. Reference has been made on pp 50-51 to Sir Charles Turner's achievement of riding a pony ten miles and over thirty leaps in forty-seven minutes, and to the conveyance of news from

Holyhead to London by relays of ponies at the
rate of twenty miles an hour

Whyte, in his *History of the British Turf,*
states that in April, 1734, a mare, 13 hands
3 inches high, belonging to Mr. Daniel Croker,
travelled 300 miles on Newmarket Heath in
64 hours 20 minutes, she had been backed to
perform the journey in 72 hours, and therefore
completed her task with 7 hours 40 minutes
to spare. Her best day's work was done on
Tuesday, April 23rd. Mr. Whyte gives the
following details of this extraordinary performance · " 24 miles and baited, 24 miles
and baited ; 24 miles and baited, 36 miles
without baiting, total 108 miles. On the
Monday and Wednesday she covered 96 miles
each day She was ridden throughout by a
boy who scaled 4 stone 1 lb. without reckoning
saddle and bridle "

Another performance worth citing as proof
of pony endurance was Sir Teddy's race with
the London mail coach to Exeter, a distance
of 172 miles. Sir Teddy, a 12 hands pony,
was led between two horses all the way, and
carried no rider himself. He performed the
journey in 23 hours 20 minutes, beating the
coach by 59 minutes.

We generally find that great feats of endurance, involving capacity to thrive on poor
and scanty food, have been accomplished

by ponies * In the Nile Campaign of 1885
the 19th Hussars were mounted on Syrian
Arabs, averaging 14 hands, which had been
purchased in Syria and Lower Egypt at an
average price of £18 The weight carried
was reduced as much as possible in view of
the hard work required of the ponies, but each
of the 350 on which the Hussars were mounted
carried about 14 stone. Their march from
Korti to Metammeh as part of a flying column
showed what these little horses could do, between the 8th and 20th of January, both days
included, they travelled 336 miles, halting on
the 13th.

On the return March from Dongola to Wady
Halfa, 250 miles, after nearly nine months'
hard work on poor food, they averaged 16 miles
a day, with one halt of two days Colonel
Barrow, in reviewing the work performed by
these ponies, says: " Food was often very
limited, and during the desert march water
was very scarce Under these conditions I
venture to think that the performances of the
regiment on the Arab ponies will compare
with the performance of any horsemen on
record "†

---

* See *Small Horses in Warfare*, by Sir Walter Gilbey,
Bart Vinton and Co , Ltd 1900
† *The XIXth and Their Times*, by Colonel John Bid-
dulph. Murray 1899

Captain Fred Burnaby, in his well-known work *A Ride to Khiva*, bears witness to the wonderful endurance of a 14 hands Tartar pony which he purchased with misgivings for £5, in default of any better mount. The animal, he tells us, was in such miserable condition, his men complained among themselves that it would not be worth *eating*, as they looked upon the little beast as foredoomed from the moment Captain Burnaby mounted it. Yet this pony, its ordinary diet supplemented by a few pounds of barley daily, carried its rider, who weighed 20 stone in his heavy sheepskin clothes, safely and well over 900 miles of bad roads, often through deep snow, and always in bitterly cold weather, the thermometer being frequently many degrees below zero. On the concluding day of the return journey this pony galloped the last 17 miles in 1 hour 25 minutes

It would be easy to multiply examples of pony endurance ; but we forbear.

The greater stamina of the pony is evidenced in another direction, namely, length of life. Instances in which ponies have attained to a great age are more numerous than those recorded of horses, and further the pony's working life is longer.

Mr. Edmund F Dease, of Gaulstown, co.

Westmeath, lost a pony in December, 1894,
which had reached the age of 39 years ; in
1896, Mrs Pratt, of Low Pond House, Bedale,
Yorks, lost a pony mare aged 45 years , on
Christmas Day, 1863, there died at Silworthy,
near Clovelly in North Devon, a pony which
had arrived within a few weeks of his sixtieth
year   Accounts of ponies which lived, and in
some cases worked, until they reached 40, 38,
37, and 35 years also recur to mind

There is a degree of cold beyond which the
horse cannot exist , and as he approaches the
latitude where the limit prevails, the effect of
climate is apparent in his conformation
The frozen and ungenial country of Lapland
has its small ponies , they are employed in
drawing sledges over the snow and transporting
forage and merchandise, which in summer are
conveyed in boats   In Iceland the pony is
dwarfed to a Liliputian size , and thriving in
the comparatively mild climate of the Shetlands we find a pony smaller than any other
in the British Islands.

It would seem from the facts it has been
possible to collect that the New Forest, Welsh,
Exmoor and Dartmoor, Fell and Connemara
breeds of ponies are in their natural state
of small value to man, though they owe to

Engraved by F. Babbage.

THE FIRST LEAP.

From the picture by Sir EDWIN LANDSEER, R.A.

the natural conditions under which they exist qualities which may be turned to very valuable account by judicious crossing with breeds of a recognised stamp.

Improvement must involve partial sacrifice of qualities, such as ability to withstand exposure and cold on insufficient food, sure-footedness, and the sagacity which avoids bog and treacherous ground. These qualities, in their highest development, are indispensable to a wild animal ; but the improved pony obtained by crossing is not destined for a wild life on the hills and wastes, and is less dependent upon them.

Partial loss of such attributes, therefore, is a price well worth paying for the increased size and better conformation which render the produce suitable for man's service with the more artificial and luxurious conditions of life inseparable from complete domesticity.

The remarkable soundness of limb and constitution, developed by the centuries of free life on the hills, are enduring qualities which appear in generation after generation of stock descended on one side from the half-wild breeds , and these are the qualities which above all it is desirable to breed into our horses of all sizes and for all purposes. The advantage to be gained by systematic improve-ment of these wild breeds of ponies is there-

fore not by any means advantageous to one
side only.

The Polo Pony Society at their meeting
of December 7th, 1898, resolved to set apart
a section of their Stud Book for the registra-
tion of Welsh, Exmoor, New Forest and
other breeds of ponies, and with reference
to this step Lord Arthur Cecil, in his Introduction to the fifth (1899) volume of the *Polo
Pony Stud Book*, says :—

"It is in the limit of height that the greatest difficulty
of the Society lies. Could we be certain of breeding
every animal between 14 hands and 14 hands 2 inches
our course would be tolerably clear. . . . There is
always, however, the danger that the best-looking and
best-nourished of our young stock will, if some means
be not found to prevent it, exceed this limit. The
remedy is more or less within our reach by utilising the
hardy little stocks of ponies which are to be found
almost indigenous in those districts of the British Isles
where there are large tracts of mountain or moorland
ground   I refer to such ponies as those found in North
and South Wales, the New Forest, Exmoor, Dartmoor,
and the hills of the North of England and West Coast
of Scotland . . .   Perhaps it may not be out of
place to mention that the present is not an inappropriate
time for upholding the breeding of ponies on hill lands
The keeping of hill sheep is not so remunerative as of
yore, the price of wool being so low and the demand for
four-year-old mutton not being anything like what it
was a few years ago , whereas, on the other hand, the
demand for ponies, especially good ones, is likely to
increase, and if farmers will only give them a fair
chance they will amply repay them for their keep up
to three years old   It is hoped that by careful consideration of their various characteristics, and by

registering such of them as are likely to breed riding
ponies, and by periodically going back to this fountain-
head of all ponies, we may be able to regulate the size
of our higher-class riding ponies to the desired limit,
while at the same time we shall infuse into their blood
the hardiness of constitution and endurance, combined
with a fiery yet even temper, so pre-eminently characteristic of the British native breeds."

The Shetland pony is the only breed to
which the quotation above does not apply, for
the reason, given on p. 108, that his value
arises from his small size and the strength so
disproportionately great.

BREEDING POLO PONIES.

Any advice on breeding ponies for Polo must necessarily be based on the broad principles of breeding generally.

The increasing popularity of the game of Polo has naturally produced an increased demand for suitable ponies; and since players hold really good Polo ponies worth almost any price, their value has risen to a level which compels attention to their breeding.

It was difficult to find ponies when an elastic 14 hands limit was the rule; and if we may judge from the prices which have been paid since the regulation height was raised to 14 hands 2 inches, the greater latitude thus afforded players in selecting mounts has done little or nothing towards solving the difficulty.

What is this Polo pony for which a fancy price is so readily forthcoming? In the first place, it is not a pony at all, but a small horse, and before the question of his education is considered at all it is necessary that the animal shall fulfil certain conditions. He must be speedy, sound and docile, he must have also courage, strength to carry weight, and staying power.

These are the qualities at which the breeder must aim , and as the necessary speed and courage are rarely to be found apart from blood the first-class pony must have what is commonly called " breeding," and this must be obtained either from the small Thoroughbred, or from the original parent of the English racehorse—the Arab or the Barb

Hence a serious difficulty faces the breeder at the outset For generations we have devoted all our care to increasing the height of the racehorse, and with such success that in 200 years we have raised his average stature by nearly 8 inches.

Mention was made in the earlier pages of this book of the statement of the great authority, Admiral Rous ,* it may be repeated here that the Admiral, writing in the year 1860, showed that the English racehorse had increased in height an inch in every twenty-five years since the year 1700 We now regard a Thoroughbred as under size if he stand less than 15 hands 3 inches. This is an important point to bear in mind ; for if

* *Baily's Magazine*, April, 1860, "The English Race-horse," II.

we are to breed Thoroughbred ponies of 14 hands 2 inches, it is plain that we must undo most that our fathers and ancestors have done.

This matter of height is not the only difficulty ; we have obtained the superior height and speed that distinguish our modern racehorses at the cost of the qualities which made the racehorses of a hundred years ago invaluable for crossing purposes

Such a Thoroughbred as Gimcrack, 14 hands $0\frac{1}{4}$ inches in height, speedy, able to carry weight and travel a distance, would be the perfect pony sire were he alive to-day The original of this portrait, painted by the celebrated horse painter George Stubbs, when the horse was at the stud, is in the possession of the Earl of Rosebery .

The modern racehorse measuring 16 hands is considered to have accomplished a wonderful feat if he win a two-mile handicap carrying 9 stone 7 lbs. The aim of breeders for years has been to produce a long-striding horse which can carry a light weight over a short distance ; and they have succeeded so well that a stout thoroughbred is a rarity.

In the modern racehorse the courage and speed remain, and for these essential qualities we look to the small Thoroughbred to help us in developing the pony able to carry 12 or 14 stone in first-class Polo.

The work which the Polo pony is called
upon to perform, though not long continued,
taxes his powers more severely than the work
demanded of any other horse in any department of sport, luxury, or utility. It is only
necessary to watch a single "period" in a
tournament match to see that the incessant
twisting and turning, sudden stopping while at
full speed and starting at a moment's notice
at top speed, varied with bursts of smart
galloping, must take an immense deal out of
the stoutest pony

Polo players should congratulate themselves
on the possibility of getting at all such animals
with a direct strain of Thoroughbred blood
in their veins. For generations all the endeavours of breeders have been devoted to
the evolution of an animal totally different
from the Polo pony which it is now desired
to produce.

So far the physical qualities of the Polo
pony have been chiefly dealt with It must be
borne in mind that when a pony, measuring
14 hands 2 inches, of the required make and
shape, has been found, he has still to be made a
Polo pony. To breed a pony of suitable size
and shape is one thing , it is quite another to
make him into a Polo pony

We frequently hear men talk of breeding
hunters. Horses of suitable make and shape

from which hunters may be *made* are bred ,
but these are not hunters until they have been
made.   Who ever heard of a fancy price being
given for a horse which, having all the physical
qualities required, had not been made clever,
which had not been schooled over country, and
had not been *proved* as a hunter ?

Those who give 200 guineas to 500 guineas
and even more for a hunter do so only on the
strength of ascertained facts concerning the
horse ; they know him to be a brilliant and
safe performer across country , a horse on
which they can depend   No man can
seriously call a horse "a hunter" until he
has been schooled and regularly hunted

The same reasoning applies to a pony.
However well shaped and handsome, however
suitable for polo he appears to be, the best bred
and best made animal cannot be described
as a " Polo pony " until he has passed through
the hands of the trainer and has shown his
fitness for a place in the polo ground in the
hands of a good player who has *proved* him

The horse may possess the qualities necessary to make him a hunter, and the pony may
possess the qualities that will make him a Polo
pony, but until each has been educated for
his work—until each has been "made"—
neither is entitled to be called by the name
which ensures a long price being paid for him

Only a trainer of experience could tell us
how many of the likely-looking animals that
come into his hands are worth the trouble of
educating

Herein we find the reason for the vast
difference in value which exists between a
pony that is untrained and one which has
gone through the various stages of stick-and-
ball practice, the bending courses, practice
games, and has finally been proven in matches

In the raw state the best-looking 14 hands
2 inches pony is worth £35 to £55. When
trained and has proved that he *is* a Polo pony,
and does not merely look like one, he is
worth many hundreds

To return to the question of breeding it
is doubtful whether owners of the best ponies
now used on English polo grounds know for
certain how the animals were bred On the
contrary, there are many high-class ponies
concerning whose pedigrees their owners know
nothing, glad though they would be to learn
particulars.

The absence of knowledge concerning the
pedigrees of these animals renders them of
little use towards helping us to decide how
we may set about breeding ponies like them.
Whether such knowledge would be useful if
it could be procured is another matter So
many different qualities must be combined in

10

the one pony to make him a polo pony that
the perfect article must be regarded as a
fortunate accident.

And while we make the English pony which
can carry weight our ideal, we acknowledge
the difficulty of procuring it by seeking other
ponies in every corner of the horse-breeding
world. Arabs and their near allies—Egyptian,
Syrian and Barb ponies, Australian, Argentine, Canadian and Cossack ponies; ponies
from the Tarbes district of France; ponies
from Texas, Wyoming and Montana—all
these have been imported and are played on
English polo grounds, and though not considered equal in speed, bottom, and courage
to the English pony, the best of them when
"made" are good enough to command high,
if not extravagant prices

The first great object, it is granted once for
all, is to get a pony with speed, handiness,
courage and stamina, for none other is good
enough to play in the best class of game. At
the same time, a large and representative
proportion of players, while heartily granting
the superiority of the English pony when it
can be obtained, recognise that, for the present
at all events, the home-bred supply is not
sufficient to meet the demand.

If it be a choice between an utterly in-
adequate supply of English-bred ponies with

blood, speed, stamina and weight-carrying power, to be bought only at prices which reserve them to the wealthiest, and a sufficiency of ponies with a strain of alien blood, somewhat less speedy, courageous and enduring, the latter must be chosen, and the Polo Pony Stud Book Society has recognised this by opening sections of their Stud Book for suitable individuals among our forest and moorland breeds, with a view of obtaining foundation stock.

In this connection it may be suggested that Polo players who are debarred by the expense from taking part in games played on full-sized ponies might combine to carry out the sensible and practical suggestion made by Mr E Sawrey-Cookson in a letter on " Polo and the Price of Ponies," which was published in *Baily's Magazine* for November, 1902 Mr. Sawrey-Cookson writes —

" I feel sure it will readily be admitted that the expense of the game is mainly attributable to the high price of the ponies, and thus it is rendered possible only to those few who can afford to pay for them ; whereas, could the cost of playing be lessened, hundreds of men who now-a-days only speak of polo as ' a good game ' would play it, and its sterling value as a game of skill and as a test of horsemanship would very soon be universally acknowledged Having myself played the game all over the world under all climates and almost all conditions, I can say, and defy contradiction, that it is possible to have just as good a game on 13 hands to 13 hands 2 inch ponies of the Exmoor or small Welsh breed as on first-class animals, provided always that the ponies engaged in such game are *all* about the same class And it is this matter of *classes* that I would commend to the earnest consideration of all those interested in the development of the game of polo Whether from players', breeders', or dealers' point of view, if the game is classed and divided in No I , II and III Class, the result would be beneficial to all "

The proposition made well deserves the attention of those who are devoting attention to the improvement of our native breeds The institution of second- and third-class polo, or let us say of 13 hands 2 inches to 14 hands, and of 13 hands to 13 hands 2 inches, polo, would not only bring many new players but would create at once a demand for ponies easily now obtainable, and would afford valuable opportunity of measuring the aptitude of particular strains for the game

Returning to our main theme, we may take it as an axiom in our endeavour to produce a breed of 14 hands 2 inches Polo ponies that the sire must be a small Thoroughbred, or, if not a Thoroughbred, an Arab.

It was the Arab and his near ally, the Barb, that laid the foundation of our Thoroughbreds in England, as shown in a previous chapter The best horses on the Turf of to-day may be traced to one of the three famous sires---the Byerly Turk, imported in 1689, the Darley Arabian in 1706, and the Godolphin Arabian

ARAB HORSE MESAOUD, 14·2 hands.

The property of Mr. WILFRED SCAWEN BLUNT.

in 1730; all of them, it may be repeated,
horses of 14 hands or very little more

There is, indeed, much to be said in favour
of the policy of returning to the original
Eastern stock to find suitable sires for our
proposed breed of 14 hands 2 inches ponies
While we have been breeding the Thoroughbred for speed, and speed only, Arab breeders
have continued to breed for stoutness, endurance, and good looks.

By going to Arab stock for our sires we
might, at the beginning, sacrifice some measure
of speed; but what was lost in that respect
would be more than compensated by the
soundness of constitution and limb which are
such conspicuous traits in the Eastern horse.
Furthermore, the difficulty of size, which first
of all confronts us in the Thoroughbred sire,
is much diminished if we adopt the Arab as
our foundation sire

We need not consider the game as played
by Orientals. The Manipuris, whose national
game it is, and from whom Europeans first
learned it, use ponies which do not often
exceed 12 hands in height The game was
introduced into India proper in 1864,* and
was first played in England by the officers of

* *Recollections of my Life*, by Sir Joseph Fayrer,
Bart. 1900.

the 10th Hussars in the year 1870, on their return from service in the East.

In India, where the game of polo was first played by Englishmen, the Arab is thought the perfect pony, the more so because the height of ponies played under the Indian Polo Association's code of rules must not exceed 13 hands 3 inches

The extensive operations of the Civil Veterinary Department in India have proved again the truth that no sire impresses more certainly and more markedly his likeness upon his stock than the Arab, a fact which is due to the high antiquity, and therefore "fixed" character, of the breed.

If, therefore, we find the stock got by the Thoroughbred sire too prone to outgrow the limit of height, we may, without self-reproach, turn for assistance to the Eastern stock, from which we have evolved the modern racehorse, as in doing so we shall simply be going a step farther back, and thereby avoid in great measure the difficulty of stature which our fathers and ancestors have created for us in our endeavour to breed a small, compact horse from the pure strain.

The next point that presents itself is, on what sort of animal would it be most advisable to cross our Thoroughbred or Arab? In the absence of any long-continued series of experi-

ments, which alone could have led to definite
results in the production of a fixed type of
pony, or a stamp of pony worth trying to
perpetuate as a fixed type, the answer must
be conjectural, we can only deal in proba-
bilities.

We may not be able to establish a breed of
which a specimen exceeding 14 hands 2 inches
shall be something quite abnormal ; on the
contrary, the whole course of experience in
breeding horses of whatever class goes to
prove the impossibility of ensuring that the
progeny of any given sire and dam shall attain
to a specified height, neither less nor more.
Nevertheless, there seems no reason why skill
and care in breeding should not in course of
time produce an animal whose *average* height
at maturity shall be the desired 14 hands
2 inches.

There are, it must be repeated, several
essential points to be kept clearly in view in
our endeavour to develop a Polo pony on the
foundation of Thoroughbred or Arab blood.
We have primarily to guard against the
tendency to exceed the regulation height, and
we must seek means to obtain the bone and
stamina which are so necessary.

Our forest and moorland mares suggest
themselves as the material at once suitable for
the purpose and easily obtainable. In these

ponies we have the small size which will
furnish the needful corrective to overgrowth,
and we have also that hardiness of constitution
and soundness of limb which are invaluable in
laying the foundation of a breed of 14 hands
2 inches ponies

Many attempts have been made from time
to time to improve these breeds, indeed, some
have been so frequently crossed with outside
blood that the purity of the strain has nearly
disappeared; this is believed to be the case
with the Dartmoor pony. At the same time
these infusions of blood have done nothing
to impair the value of the ponies in respect
of their intrinsic qualities of hardiness and
soundness

That small Thoroughbred and Arab blood
blends well with the forest and moorland
strains has been abundantly proved, the
thoroughbred horse Marske, sire of Eclipse,
who was under 14 hands 2 inches, as is recorded, stood at service in the New Forest
district for three or four seasons from about
the year 1765, and produced upon the New
Forest breed a beneficial effect which remained
in evidence for many years

The late Prince Consort sent a grey Arab
stallion to stand at New Park, which did much
good in improving the stamp of pony, and in
1889, as before mentioned, Her Majesty lent

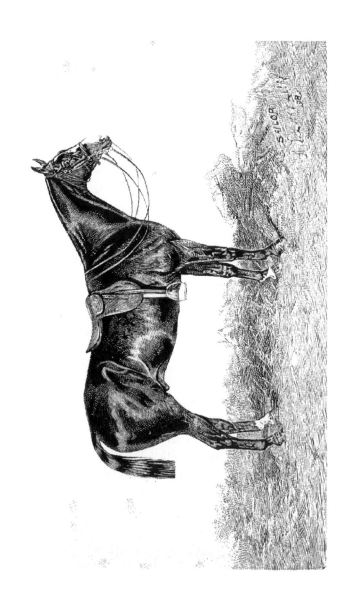

two Arab sires, which remained respectively
for two and three seasons and produced a
marked effect on the forest breed. One of
the Dongola Arabs or Barbs which Mr.
Knight used gave the best results on the
Exmoor ponies, and the use of the thoroughbred horses, Pandarus, by Whalebone, and
Canopus, grandson of "Velocipede," also
contributed to increase the size of the breed.

Some of the best hunters in the West of
England trace their descent on the dam's side
to the Welsh Mountain pony, the sire of some
of the best horses, however, being a horse with
a stain in his pedigree, viz., Ellesmere by New
Oswestry. In this connection it may be remarked that Bright Pearl, winner in the class
for unmade Polo ponies at the Crystal Palace
Pony Show, held in July, 1899, was got by
the thoroughbred Pearl Diver out of a Welsh
Hill Pony mare whose wonderful jumping
powers had gained her many prizes.

The fact that the forest and moorland
breeds owe their small size to the rigorous
conditions of a natural free life and the spare
diet accessible must not be lost sight of, for
their tendency to increase in size when taken
up, sheltered and well fed is very marked.
The fact is of importance, because we could
not expect that foals got by a thoroughbred
or Arab sire would possess the stamina that

11

enables the forest or moorland pony to withstand exposure.

It is also said that the stock got by Marske
throve under the comparatively mild rigours
of New Forest life, but the Thoroughbred
of 135 years ago was a smaller, stouter and
hardier animal than is his descendant of to-
day. It would therefore be necessary to
choose between losing the young half-bred
stock altogether, and of rearing it under more
or less artificial conditions with the certainty
of rearing an animal which would respond to
those conditions by increased stature.

The same remarks apply equally to stock
got from forest or moorland mares by an
Arab or Barb sire, which flourish in a warm
and dry climate, unlike the variable moist
climate of England.

Judgment and care might do something to
obviate the tendency to overgrowth, the happy
medium to adopt would be to allow the dams
with their half-bred youngsters as much liberty
as varying climatic conditions indicated the
well-being of the latter could withstand

The mares which have finished their active
career of four or five seasons on the polo
ground might with advantage be used for
breeding purposes, animals which have been
played in first-class matches and are known
to possess good mouths, good temper, good

manners and speed, have much to recommend
them as dams; for these essential qualities
are likely to be inherited by their progeny.

It is reasonable to think that a breed
of small horses can be established by the
judicious intermingling of our forest or moorland mares with small Thoroughbred or Arab
sires. Experience in stock-raising has taught
breeders that the creation of a new and
improved strain, whether of horses, cattle,
sheep or swine, is a slow process, though
success has been achieved in the end.

That a breed of, we will not say Polo ponies,
but riding ponies of the right stamp to educate
for polo can be evolved and established there
is no reason to doubt. The aim for the
future must be to establish a breed which
shall reproduce itself without the assistance
of correctives in the shape of resort to
Thoroughbred, Arab, or Barb blood.

Not one hundred years ago cattle imported
from Holland were called " Shorthorn or
Dutch", and the direct descendants of these
cattle are our famous Shorthorns. Numerous
other breeds of stock have been established
during the past century. Among the number
the breeds of sheep known as the Hampshire,
the Shropshire and the Oxford Down.

These breeds were only produced after many
endeavours and many failures; and with the

successes of past days to encourage him, the breeder of ponies who aims at the establishment of a fixed type of any given character need not despair of achieving his purpose.

All the breeder can do is to determine the foundations upon which he believes the future breed of riding pony may be established, whether upon the Thoroughbred or on the Thoroughbred's original ancestor, the Arab, and exercise his best care and judgment in mating and rearing.

It may be that the present generation will lay the foundation of a breed of 14 hands 2 inches riding ponies, and that posterity will build the edifice and enjoy the benefits

Works by SIR WALTER GILBEY, Bart.,
Published by Vinton & Co., 9 New Bridge Street, London, E.C.

Modern Carriages *Published April, 1904*
The passenger vehicles now in use, with notes on their origin Illustrations
Octavo, cloth gilt, price 2s net, post free, 2s 3d

Poultry-Keeping on Farms and Small Holdings *Published 1904*
Being a practical treatise on the production of Poultry and Eggs for the Market
By Sir WALTER GILBEY, Bart Illustrated Price 2s , post free, 2s 3d

Early Carriages and Roads *Published 1903*
In this publication attention has been given to the early history of wheeled convey-
ances in England and their development up to recent times With Seventeen
Illustrations Octavo, cloth gilt, price 2s net, post free 2s 4d

Thoroughbred and Other Ponies *Published 1903*
With Remarks on the Height of Racehorses since 1700 Being a Revised and
Enlarged Edition of PONIES PAST AND PRESENT With Ten Illustrations
Octavo, cloth gilt price 5s net , post free, 5s 4d

Hunter Sires *Published 1903*
Suggestions for Breeding Hunters, Troopers and General-Purpose Horses By
I Sir WALTER GILBEY Bart II CHARLES W TINDALL III Right Hon
FREDERICK W WRENCH IV W T TRENCH Octavo, paper covers, 6d , post
free 7d

Horses for the Army—a suggestion *Published 1902*
Octavo, paper covers, 6d

Horse-breeding in England and India, and Army Horses
Abroad *Published 1901*
Seventeen Chapters Horse-breeding in England, Eight Chapters, Horse-breeding
Abroad , Thirteen pages, Horse-breeding in India Nine Illustrations Octavo,
cloth price 2s net, post free, 2s 3d

Riding & Driving Horses, their Breeding & Rearing *Published 1901*
An Address delivered in London on March 2 1885, and Discussion thereon by the
late Duke of Westminster, Earl Carrington Sir Nigel Kingscote, the late Mr Edmund
Tattersall, and others Reprint 1901 Octavo price 2s net, post free, 2s 3d

Small Horses in Warfare *Published 1900*
Arguments in favour of their use for light cavalry and mounted infantry Illustrated
Octavo, cloth gilt, price 2s net , post free, 2s 3d

Horses Past and Present *Published 1900*
A sketch of the History of the Horse in England from the earliest times Nine
Illustrations Octavo, cloth gilt, price 2s net , post free, 2s 3d

Animal Painters of England *Published 1900*
The lives of fifty animal painters, from the year 1650 to 1850 Illustrated
Two vols , quarto cloth gilt, Two Guineas net

The Great Horse or War Horse *Published 1899*
From the Roman Invasion till its development into the Shire Horse New and
Revised Edition, 1899 Seventeen Illustrations Octavo, cloth gilt, price 2s net ,
post free, 2s 3d

Harness Horses *Published 1898*
The scarcity of Carriage Horses and how to breed them 3rd Edition Twenty-one
Chapters Seven full-page Illustrations Octavo, cloth gilt, price 2s net, post
free, 2s 3d

Young Race Horses—suggestions *Published 1898*
for rearing, feeding and treatment Twenty-two Chapters With Frontispiece and
Diagrams Octavo, cloth gilt, price 2s. net , post free, 2s 3d

Life of George Stubbs, R A. *Published 1898*
Ten Chapters Twenty-six Illustrations and Headpieces Quarto, whole Morocco,
gilt, £3 3s net

X

|

Lightning Source UK Ltd.
Milton Keynes UK
UKHW020759010822
406672UK00006B/636